JOHN
MACARTHUR

ACTS

The Spread of the Gospel

THOMAS NELSON

Since 1798

NASHVILLE   DALLAS   MEXICO CITY   RIO DE JANEIRO   BEIJING

ACTS
MACARTHUR BIBLE STUDIES

John MacArthur
"Unleashing God's Truth, One Verse at at a Time®."
"Unleashing God's Truth, One Verse at a Time" is a trademark of Grace to You. All rights reserved.

Published in Nashville, Tennessee, by Thomas Nelson. Thomas Nelson is a registered trademark of Thomas Nelson, Inc.

Thomas Nelson, Inc. titles may be purchased in bulk for education, business, fundraising, or sales promotional use. For information, please email SpecialMarkets@ThomasNelson.com.

Published in association with the literary agency of Wolgemuth & Associates, Inc.

Produced with the assistance of the Livingstone Corporation. Project staff include Jake Barton, Betsy Todt Schmitt, and Andy Culbertson. Project editors: Mary Horner Collins, Amber Rae, and Len Woods

Scripture quotations marked NKJV are taken from the The New King James Version®. © 1982 by Thomas Nelson, Inc. Used by permission. All rights reserved.

"Keys to the Text" material taken from the following sources:

Anxiety Attacked. © 1993, 1996 by John MacArthur, Jr. Published by Victor Books, Wheaton, Illinois. Used by permission.

The God Who Loves. © 1996, 2003 by John MacArthur. Published by Thomas Nelson Publishers.

The MacArthur Study Bible (electronic ed.), John MacArthur, General Editor. © 1997 by Word Publishing. All rights reserved. Used by permission.

Nelson's New Illustrated Bible Dictionary, Rev. ed. R. F. Youngblood, F. F. Bruce, R. K. Harrison, editors. © 1995 by Thomas Nelson Publishers. Used by permission.

Acts. MacArthur Commentary Series. © 2000 by John MacArthur. Published by Moody Press, Chicago, Illinois. Used by permission.

What Does the Bible Say About—? Nelson's A to Z series. © 2001 by Thomas Nelson Publishers.

Cover Art by Kirk Luttrell, Livingstone Corporation
Interior Design and Composition by Joel Bartlett, Livingstone Corporation

ISBN: 978-1-4185-0874-6

Printed in the United States of America.

13 14 15 QG 26

Contents

INTRODUCTION TO ACTS

As the second book Luke addressed to Theophilus (see Luke 1:3), Acts may originally have had no title. The Greek manuscripts title the book "Acts," and many add "of the Apostles." The Greek word translated "Acts" (*praxeis*) was often used to describe the achievements of great people. Acts does feature the notable figures in the early years of the church, especially Peter (chapters 1–12) and Paul (chapters 13–28). But the book could more properly be called "The Acts of the Holy Spirit through the Apostles," since His sovereign, superintending work was far more significant than that of any human being. The Spirit directed, controlled, and empowered the church and caused it to grow in numbers, spiritual power, and influence.

AUTHOR AND DATE

Since Luke's Gospel was the first book addressed to Theophilus (Luke 1:3), it is logical to conclude that Luke is also the author of Acts, although he is not named in either book. The writings of the early church fathers such as Irenaeus, Clement of Alexandria, Tertullian, Origen, Eusebius, and Jerome affirm Luke's authorship, and so does the Muratorian Canon (ca. AD 170). Because he is a relatively obscure figure, mentioned only three times in the New Testament (Col. 4:14; 2 Tim. 4:11; Philem. 24), it is unlikely that anyone would have forged a work to make it appear to be Luke's. A forger surely would have attributed the work to a more prominent person.

Luke was Paul's close friend, traveling companion, and personal physician (Col. 4:14). He was a careful researcher (Luke 1:1–4) and an accurate historian, displaying an intimate knowledge of Roman laws and customs, as well as the geography of Palestine, Asia Minor, and Italy. In writing Acts, Luke drew on written sources (15:23–29; 23:26–30), and he also, no doubt, interviewed key figures, such as Peter, John, and others in the Jerusalem church. Paul's two-year imprisonment at Caesarea (24:27) gave Luke ample opportunity to interview Philip and his daughters (who were considered important sources of information on the early days of the church). Finally, Luke's frequent use of the first-person plural pronouns "we" and "us" (16:10–17; 20:5–21:18; 27:1–28:16) reveals that he was an eyewitness to many of the events recorded in Acts.

Some believe Luke wrote Acts after the fall of Jerusalem (AD 70; his death was probably in the mid-eighties). It is more likely, however, that he wrote much earlier, before the end of Paul's first Roman imprisonment (ca. AD 60–62). That date is the most natural explanation for the abrupt ending of Acts, which leaves Paul awaiting trial before Caesar. Surely Luke, who devoted more than half of Acts to Paul's ministry, would have stated the outcome of that trial and described Paul's subsequent ministry, second imprisonment (2 Tim. 4:11), and death, if those events had happened before he wrote Acts. Luke's silence about such notable events as the martyrdom of James, head of the Jerusalem church (AD 62, according to the Jewish historian Josephus), the persecution under Nero (AD 64), and the fall of Jerusalem (AD 70) also suggests he wrote Acts before those events transpired.

BACKGROUND AND SETTING

As Luke makes clear in the prologue to his Gospel, he wrote to give Theophilus (and the others who would read his work) "a narrative of those things" (Luke 1:1) that Jesus had accomplished during His earthly ministry. Accordingly, Luke wrote in his Gospel "an orderly account" (Luke 1:3) of those momentous events. Acts continues that record, noting what Jesus accomplished through the early church. Beginning with Jesus' ascension, through the birth of the church on the Day of Pentecost, to Paul's preaching at Rome, Acts chronicles the spread of the gospel (the good news of Jesus) and the growth of the church. It also records the mounting opposition to the gospel.

Theophilus, whose name means "lover of God," is unknown to history apart from his mention in Luke and Acts. Whether he was a believer whom Luke was instructing or a pagan whom Luke sought to convert is not known. Luke's address of him as "most excellent Theophilus" (Luke 1:3) suggests that he was a Roman official of some importance (24:3; 26:25).

HISTORICAL AND THEOLOGICAL THEMES

As the first work of church history ever penned, Acts records the initial response to the Great Commission (Matt. 28:19–20). It provides information on the first three decades of the church's existence—material found nowhere else in the New Testament. Though not primarily a doctrinal work, Acts nonetheless emphasizes that Jesus of Nazareth was Israel's long-awaited Messiah, shows that the gospel is offered to all people (not merely the Jews), and stresses the work of the Holy Spirit (mentioned more than fifty times). Acts also makes frequent use of the Old Testament: for example, 2:17–21 (Joel 2:28–32); 2:25–28 (Ps. 16:8–11); 2:35 (Ps. 110:1); 4:11 (Ps. 118:22); 4:25–26 (Ps. 2:1–2); 7:49–50 (Isa. 66:1–2); 8:32–33 (Isa. 53:7–8); 28:26–27 (Isa. 6:9–10).

Acts abounds with transitions: from the ministry of Jesus to that of the apostles; from the old covenant to the new covenant; from Israel as God's witness nation to the church (composed of both Jews and Gentiles) as God's witness people. The book of Hebrews sets forth the theology of the transition from the old covenant to the new; Acts depicts the new covenant's practical outworking in the life of the church.

THE BIRTH OF THE CHURCH

DRAWING NEAR

How would you rate the reputation of Christ's church in the world today? Why?

_____

_____

_____

THE CONTEXT

Luke's book of Acts picks up where his Gospel left off, providing details of the birth and early years of the church that Jesus had promised to build. Together, the two books, Luke and Acts, form a comprehensive and seamless account of how the followers of Jesus "turned the world upside down" (Acts 17:6) by taking the good news of the life, death, and resurrection of Jesus Christ to "the end of the earth" (Acts 1:8).

The opening chapters of Acts portray the apostles and other disciples gathered together in Jerusalem just before the feast of Pentecost. Following Christ's ascension into heaven and a season of prayer, the time comes for the fulfillment of the promise of the indwelling Spirit (see John 14:16–17, 26; 16:5–15). This marvelous, miraculous outpouring of God results in the birth of the church and provides the supernatural power for believers to take the life-changing message of the gospel to all nations. Acts 2 concludes with a snapshot of church life in the first century.

KEYS TO THE TEXT

Holy Spirit: The Holy Spirit is the divine agent who creates, sustains, and preserves spiritual life in those who place their trust in Jesus Christ. The Holy Spirit is not merely an influence or an impersonal power emanating from God. He is a person, the third member of the Trinity, equal in every way to God the Father and God the Son. Among the many characteristics of personhood that the Holy Spirit manifests are: He functions with mind, emotion, and will; He loves the saints; He communicates with them, teaches, guides, comforts, and chastises them; He can be grieved, quenched, lied to, tested, resisted, and blasphemed. Since Pentecost, the Holy Spirit has indwelt all believers, illuminating their understanding and application of God's Word. He fills them, seals them, communes with them, fellowships with them, intercedes for them, comforts them, admonishes them, sanctifies them, and enables them to resist sin and serve God.

Unleashing the Text

Read 1:1–2:47, noting the key words and definitions next to the passage.

Acts 1:1–2:47 (NKJV)

the former account (v. 1)—the Gospel of Luke

He was taken up (v. 2)— Christ's ascension to the Father

forty days (v. 3)—the time period between Christ's death and His ascension

wait for the Promise of the Father (v. 4)—Jesus repeatedly promised that God would send His followers the Holy Spirit.

restore the kingdom to Israel (v. 6)—The apostles still believed the earthly form of the Messiah's kingdom was imminent.

receive power (v. 8)—a new dimension or divine enabling for witness

witnesses (v. 8)—The English word "martyr" comes from this Greek word; it designates one who tells the truth about Christ (which often resulted in death).

1 *The former account I made, O Theophilus, of all that Jesus began both to do and teach,*

2 *until the day in which He was taken up, after He through the Holy Spirit had given commandments to the apostles whom He had chosen,*

3 *to whom He also presented Himself alive after His suffering by many infallible proofs, being seen by them during forty days and speaking of the things pertaining to the kingdom of God.*

4 *And being assembled together with them, He commanded them not to depart from Jerusalem, but to wait for the Promise of the Father, "which," He said, "you have heard from Me;*

5 *for John truly baptized with water, but you shall be baptized with the Holy Spirit not many days from now."*

6 *Therefore, when they had come together, they asked Him, saying, "Lord, will You at this time restore the kingdom to Israel?"*

7 *And He said to them, "It is not for you to know times or seasons which the Father has put in His own authority.*

8 *But you shall receive power when the Holy Spirit has come upon you; and you shall be witnesses to Me in Jerusalem, and in all Judea and Samaria, and to the end of the earth."*

9 *Now when He had spoken these things, while they watched, He was taken up, and a cloud received Him out of their sight.*

10 *And while they looked steadfastly toward heaven*

as He went up, behold, two men stood by them in white apparel,

11 who also said, "Men of Galilee, why do you stand gazing up into heaven? This same Jesus, who was taken up from you into heaven, will so come in like manner as you saw Him go into heaven."

12 Then they returned to Jerusalem from the mount called Olivet, which is near Jerusalem, a Sabbath day's journey.

13 And when they had entered, they went up into the upper room where they were staying: Peter, James, John, and Andrew; Philip and Thomas; Bartholomew and Matthew; James the son of Alphaeus and Simon the Zealot; and Judas the son of James.

14 These all continued with one accord in prayer and supplication, with the women and Mary the mother of Jesus, and with His brothers.

15 And in those days Peter stood up in the midst of the disciples (altogether the number of names was about a hundred and twenty), and said,

16 "Men and brethren, this Scripture had to be fulfilled, which the Holy Spirit spoke before by the mouth of David concerning Judas, who became a guide to those who arrested Jesus;

17 for he was numbered with us and obtained a part in this ministry."

18 (Now this man purchased a field with the wages of iniquity; and falling headlong, he burst open in the middle and all his entrails gushed out.

19 And it became known to all those dwelling in Jerusalem; so that field is called in their own language, Akel Dama, that is, Field of Blood.)

20 "For it is written in the Book of Psalms: 'Let his dwelling place be desolate, And let no one live in it'; and, 'Let another take his office.'

21 "Therefore, of these men who have accompanied us all the time that the Lord Jesus went in and out among us,

two men . . . in white apparel (v. 10)—angels in the form of men

come in like manner (v. 11)—Christ will one day return with clouds to the earth (the Mount of Olives) to set up His kingdom.

Bartholomew (v. 13)—also known as Nathanael (see John 1:45–49)

Judas, the son of James (v. 13)—also known as Thaddeus (see Mark 3:18)

brothers (v. 14)—actually half brothers

the Holy Spirit . . . by the mouth of David (v. 16)—a clear description of divine inspiration

must become a witness with us of His resurrection (v. 22) — Judas's replacement among the apostles had to be one who had participated in Jesus' earthly ministry and seen the resurrected Christ.

his own place (v. 25)—a way of saying that Judas chose his own fate by rejecting Christ

cast their lots (v. 26)—a common Old Testament method of determining God's will; no longer necessary after the coming of the Holy Spirit

Pentecost (2:1)—the Feast of Weeks or Harvest, celebrated fifty days after Passover

mighty wind (v. 2)—a frequent scriptural picture of the Spirit

tongues, as of fire (v. 3)—a symbolic indicator of the divine presence

with other tongues (v. 4)—known languages, not ecstatic utterances

speak in his own language (v. 6)—These pilgrims in Jerusalem were hearing the Galilean disciples speaking about the wonderful works of God (see verse 11) in their native dialects—an astonishing miracle.

22 beginning from the baptism of John to that day when He was taken up from us, one of these must become a witness with us of His resurrection."

23 And they proposed two: Joseph called Barsabas, who was surnamed Justus, and Matthias.

24 And they prayed and said, "You, O Lord, who know the hearts of all, show which of these two You have chosen

25 to take part in this ministry and apostleship from which Judas by transgression fell, that he might go to his own place."

26 And they cast their lots, and the lot fell on Matthias. And he was numbered with the eleven apostles.

2:1 When the Day of Pentecost had fully come, they were all with one accord in one place.

2 And suddenly there came a sound from heaven, as of a rushing mighty wind, and it filled the whole house where they were sitting.

3 Then there appeared to them divided tongues, as of fire, and one sat upon each of them.

4 And they were all filled with the Holy Spirit and began to speak with other tongues, as the Spirit gave them utterance.

5 And there were dwelling in Jerusalem Jews, devout men, from every nation under heaven.

6 And when this sound occurred, the multitude came together, and were confused, because everyone heard them speak in his own language.

7 Then they were all amazed and marveled, saying to one another, "Look, are not all these who speak Galileans?

8 And how is it that we hear, each in our own language in which we were born?

9 Parthians and Medes and Elamites, those dwelling in Mesopotamia, Judea and Cappadocia, Pontus and Asia,

10 Phrygia and Pamphylia, Egypt and the parts of Libya adjoining Cyrene, visitors from Rome, both Jews and proselytes,

11 Cretans and Arabs—we hear them speaking in our own tongues the wonderful works of God."

12 So they were all amazed and perplexed, saying to one another, "Whatever could this mean?"

13 Others mocking said, "They are full of new wine."

14 But Peter, standing up with the eleven, raised his voice and said to them, "Men of Judea and all who dwell in Jerusalem, let this be known to you, and heed my words.

15 For these are not drunk, as you suppose, since it is only the third hour of the day.

16 But this is what was spoken by the prophet Joel:

17 'And it shall come to pass in the last days, says God, That I will pour out of My Spirit on all flesh; Your sons and your daughters shall prophesy, Your young men shall see visions, Your old men shall dream dreams.

18 And on My menservants and on My maidservants I will pour out My Spirit in those days; And they shall prophesy.

19 I will show wonders in heaven above And signs in the earth beneath: Blood and fire and vapor of smoke.

20 The sun shall be turned into darkness, And the moon into blood, Before the coming of the great and awesome day of the LORD.

21 And it shall come to pass That whoever calls on the name of the LORD Shall be saved.'

22 "Men of Israel, hear these words: Jesus of Nazareth, a Man attested by God to you by miracles, wonders, and signs which God did through Him in your midst, as you yourselves also know—

23 Him, being delivered by the determined purpose and foreknowledge of God, you have taken by lawless hands, have crucified, and put to death;

24 whom God raised up, having loosed the pains of death, because it was not possible that He should be held by it.

25 For David says concerning Him: 'I foresaw the LORD

---

wonderful works of God (v. 11)—probably quotations from the Old Testament

new wine (v. 13)—Some accused the disciples of being drunk.

spoken by the prophet Joel (v. 16)—a pre-fulfillment of Joel's prophecy; the Spirit will be poured out in full during Messiah's millennial kingdom

last days (v. 17)—the present era of redemptive history from the first coming of Christ all the way to His second coming

visions . . . dreams (v. 17)—a common source of revelation in the Old Testament; rare in the New Testament; they will become frequent again during the Tribulation period spoken of by Joel

signs (v. 19)—These mighty works are not an end in themselves, but they point to God and His truth.

attested . . . by miracles, wonders, and signs (v. 22)—God validated Jesus as the Messiah by the supernatural works He performed.

not possible (v. 24)—Because of his divine power and God's promise and purpose, death could not keep Jesus in the grave.

always before my face, For He is at my right hand, that I may not be shaken.

26 Therefore my heart rejoiced, and my tongue was glad; Moreover my flesh also will rest in hope.

27 For You will not leave my soul in Hades, Nor will You allow Your Holy One to see corruption.

28 You have made known to me the ways of life; You will make me full of joy in Your presence.'

29 "Men and brethren, let me speak freely to you of the patriarch David, that he is both dead and buried, and his tomb is with us to this day.

30 Therefore, being a prophet, and knowing that God had sworn with an oath to him that of the fruit of his body, according to the flesh, He would raise up the Christ to sit on his throne,

31 he, foreseeing this, spoke concerning the resurrection of the Christ, that His soul was not left in Hades, nor did His flesh see corruption.

32 This Jesus God has raised up, of which we are all witnesses.

33 Therefore being exalted to the right hand of God, and having received from the Father the promise of the Holy Spirit, He poured out this which you now see and hear.

34 "For David did not ascend into the heavens, but he says himself: 'The LORD said to my Lord, "Sit at My right hand,

35 Till I make Your enemies Your footstool."'

36 "Therefore let all the house of Israel know assuredly that God has made this Jesus, whom you crucified, both Lord and Christ."

37 Now when they heard this, they were cut to the heart, and said to Peter and the rest of the apostles, "Men and brethren, what shall we do?"

38 Then Peter said to them, "Repent, and let every one of you be baptized in the name of Jesus Christ for the remission of sins; and you shall receive the gift of the Holy Spirit.

39 For the promise is to you and to your children, and

Hades (v. 27)—the New Testament equivalent of the Old Testament grave; the general place of the dead

his tomb is with us (v. 29)—a reminder to the Jews that David was never resurrected; thus he could not be the fulfillment of the prophecy of Psalm 16

Therefore (v. 36)—Peter summarizes his sermon with a powerful statement of certainty: the Old Testament prophecies of resurrection and exaltation provide overwhelming evidence that the crucified Jesus is the promised Messiah.

cut to the heart (v. 37)—wounded, stabbed; that is, under intense spiritual conviction

Repent (v. 38)—a change of mind and purpose that turns an individual from sin to God

be baptized . . . for the remission of sins (v. 38)—be dipped or immersed in water to identify symbolically with Christ's death, burial, and resurrection; this act does not result in sins being washed away, rather it is an act of obedience to which we submit because our sins have been remitted (an alternate translation) to all who are afar off, as many as the Lord our God will call."

40 And with many other words he testified and exhorted them, saying, "Be saved from this perverse generation."

41 Then those who gladly received his word were baptized; and that day about three thousand souls were added to them.

42 And they continued steadfastly in the apostles' doctrine and fellowship, in the breaking of bread, and in prayers.

43 Then fear came upon every soul, and many wonders and signs were done through the apostles.

44 Now all who believed were together, and had all things in common,

45 and sold their possessions and goods, and divided them among all, as anyone had need.

46 So continuing daily with one accord in the temple, and breaking bread from house to house, they ate their food with gladness and simplicity of heart,

47 praising God and having favor with all the people. And the Lord added to the church daily those who were being saved.

apostles' doctrine (v. 42)—the exposition of God's revealed truth, that is, the Scripture

fellowship (v. 42)—partnership or sharing in the faith

breaking of bread (v. 42)—a reference to the Lord's Table, or Communion

all things in common (v. 44)—not communism or a redistribution of wealth, but a generous attitude in which they held possessions lightly and moved quickly to meet needs in the body

the Lord added (v. 47)—salvation is a sovereign event

1) What words and phrases does Luke use in his opening paragraph to drive home the truth of Christ's resurrection?

_____

_____

_____

2) What instructions and insights did Jesus give His followers concerning the Holy Spirit?

_____

_____

_____

(Verses to consider: Rom. 8:9; 1 Cor. 6:19–20; Tit. 3:5–6; Eph. 3:16, 20)

9

3) Following the ascension of Christ into heaven what did the believers do? What are we told about the identity of this group?

_____

_____

_____

_____

4) Use three adjectives to describe the events that occurred after the Spirit came.

_____

_____

_____

_____

GOING DEEPER

This is the beginning of the church. For more insight about what the church is, read the apostle Paul's description of the church in Ephesians 3:1–12.

EXPLORING THE MEANING

5) What theological insights does Paul's exposition in Ephesians 3 add to Luke's historical narrative of the birth of the church? What is God's intent in creating the entity we call the *church*?

_____

_____

_____

_____

6) What was the thrust of Peter's sermon to the gathered crowd at Pentecost?

_____

_____

_____

_____

7) How does Luke describe the atmosphere and activities of the first-century church (2:42–47)?

_____

_____

_____

_____

TRUTH FOR TODAY

In an effort to appeal to people's interest, the church today emphasizes a great many different programs, methods, and approaches. "Culturally relevant" worship services emphasizing music and drama have become increasingly popular. Secular psychology, management techniques, and advertising strategies have all made significant inroads into the life of the church. Seminars on everything from how to have a good marriage to how to handle money abound. Not all of those things may be harmful. Some, in their place, may even be helpful. But what has too often been sacrificed in the flurry of activities and programs is the priority of preaching. The first event of church history, following the coming of the Spirit, was Peter's sermon. It led to three thousand conversions and launched the church. The book of Acts is largely the record of apostolic preaching. Preaching has always remained central to the church's mission.

REFLECTING ON THE TEXT

8) In Acts, there is always a close connection between the activity of God's Spirit and the proclamation of the gospel. Time and again those who experience the baptism or filling of the Spirit begin immediately speaking with others the truth about God and His Son, Jesus Christ. How vocal are you about the things of God? To what do you ascribe this?

_____

_____

_____

_____

(Verses to consider: 1:8; 2:4, 17; 4:8, 31; 6:10; 10:44–46; 13:9; 19:6)

9) These early believers had no building of their own to meet in. What does that tell you about what the "church" really is?

_____

_____

_____

10) Reflect on your prayer habits (and your church's commitment to prayer). What specific, practical step can you take this week to emulate the early church in this area?

_____

_____

_____

_____

11) Write down a prayer for your church, that it might become all that God wants it to be. Ask God to make you faithful to serve, give, and pray.

_____

_____

_____

_____

PERSONAL RESPONSE

Write out additional reflections, questions you may have, or a prayer.

_____

_____

_____

_____

_____

_____

_____

—2—
THE APOSTLES OF THE CHURCH

Acts 3:1–5:42

DRAWING NEAR

As the early church grew, the new Christians were not always popular. Have you ever been disliked or laughed at for being a Christian? If so, how did it feel? How did you respond?

_____

_____

_____

THE CONTEXT

With the coming of the Spirit upon the followers of Christ, the church was born and immediately began to grow. Now we see the impact of this new program in the eternal, unfolding plan of God.

The apostles Peter and John are the initial leaders of this new entity. A healing at the temple gives them an open door to declare plainly that Jesus, crucified and resurrected, is the long-awaited Messiah who fulfills all the predictions of the prophets. Their preaching, however, quickly gets them in trouble with the Sanhedrin, the same authorities who arrested and killed Jesus, the dangerous rabbi from Nazareth. These religious leaders now seek to intimidate and silence His followers.

Undaunted, the believers pray for courage and continue living in such a way that the world sits up and takes notice. Those outside the church are startled to see believers care for one another and share with one another in extravagant ways. The apostles continue to boldly preach about Jesus right in the temple courts.

Still smarting from the apostles' refusal to heed their threats, and in light of the growing popularity of the church, the Jewish authorities clamp down. They arrest and jail Peter and his colleagues. When God miraculously frees His spokesmen in the night, the apostles march straight back to the temple and resume their preaching! Not even a severe beating at the hands of the council can dampen the fervor of the people of God.

13

KEYS TO THE TEXT

The Temple: Because these first Christians were devout Jews, they continued to meet in the temple for worship and to teach in the synagogues. This temple in Jerusalem was begun by Herod the Great in 20 BC and was still under construction when the Romans destroyed it in AD 70. At the time of Jesus' ministry and after, the temple was one of the most impressive structures in the world, made of massive blocks of stone bedecked with gold ornamentation. The temple buildings were made of gleaming white marble, and the whole eastern wall of the large main structure was covered with gold plates that reflected the morning sun, making a spectacle that was visible for miles. The entire temple mount had been enlarged by Herod's engineers, by means of large retaining walls and vaulted chambers. By this means the large courtyard area atop the temple mount was effectively doubled. The whole temple complex was magnificent by any standard.

Chief Priests, Rulers, Elders, and Scribes: These positions made up the Sanhedrin, the Jewish national ruling body and supreme court. It had seventy-one members, including the High Priest. The chief priests were a group within the Sanhedrin composed of members of influential priestly families. They were mostly Sadducees. The scribes were primarily Pharisees and were the authorities on Jewish law.

UNLEASHING THE TEXT

Read 3:1–5:42, noting the key words and definitions next to the passage.

Acts 3:1–5:42 (NKJV)

ninth hour (v. 1)—3:00 PM

alms (v. 2)—a charitable donation of money

1 Now Peter and John went up together to the temple at the hour of prayer, the ninth hour.
2 And a certain man lame from his mother's womb was carried, whom they laid daily at the gate of the temple which is called Beautiful, to ask alms from those who entered the temple;
3 who, seeing Peter and John about to go into the temple, asked for alms.
4 And fixing his eyes on him, with John, Peter said, "Look at us."
5 So he gave them his attention, expecting to receive something from them.
6 Then Peter said, "Silver and gold I do not have,

but what I do have I give you: In the name of Jesus Christ of Nazareth, rise up and walk."

7 And he took him by the right hand and lifted him up, and immediately his feet and ankle bones received strength.

8 So he, leaping up, stood and walked and entered the temple with them—walking, leaping, and praising God.

9 And all the people saw him walking and praising God.

10 Then they knew that it was he who sat begging alms at the Beautiful Gate of the temple; and they were filled with wonder and amazement at what had happened to him.

11 Now as the lame man who was healed held on to Peter and John, all the people ran together to them in the porch which is called Solomon's, greatly amazed.

porch . . . Solomon's (v. 11)—a portico surrounding the temple's Court of the Gentiles

12 So when Peter saw it, he responded to the people: "Men of Israel, why do you marvel at this? Or why look so intently at us, as though by our own power or godliness we had made this man walk?

13 The God of Abraham, Isaac, and Jacob, the God of our fathers, glorified His Servant Jesus, whom you delivered up and denied in the presence of Pilate, when he was determined to let Him go.

the God of Abraham, Isaac, and Jacob (v. 13)—a description of God familiar to Peter's Jewish audience

14 But you denied the Holy One and the Just, and asked for a murderer to be granted to you,

murderer (v. 14)—that is, Barabbas (see Mark 15:11; Luke 23:18)

15 and killed the Prince of life, whom God raised from the dead, of which we are witnesses.

Prince of life (v. 15)—the Divine Originator of life

16 And His name, through faith in His name, has made this man strong, whom you see and know. Yes, the faith which comes through Him has given him this perfect soundness in the presence of you all.

17 "Yet now, brethren, I know that you did it in ignorance, as did also your rulers.

18 But those things which God foretold by the mouth of all His prophets, that the Christ would suffer, He has thus fulfilled.

be converted (v. 19)—a frequent New Testament word that refers to sinners turning to God

19 Repent therefore and be converted, that your sins may be blotted out, so that times of refreshing may come from the presence of the Lord,

20 and that He may send Jesus Christ, who was preached to you before,

21 whom heaven must receive until the times of restoration of all things, which God has spoken by the mouth of all His holy prophets since the world began.

22 For Moses truly said to the fathers, 'The LORD your God will raise up for you a Prophet like me from your brethren. Him you shall hear in all things, whatever He says to you.

23 And it shall be that every soul who will not hear that Prophet shall be utterly destroyed from among the people.'

24 Yes, and all the prophets, from Samuel and those who follow, as many as have spoken, have also foretold these days.

25 You are sons of the prophets, and of the covenant which God made with our fathers, saying to Abraham, 'And in your seed all the families of the earth shall be blessed.'

26 To you first, God, having raised up His Servant Jesus, sent Him to bless you, in turning away every one of you from your iniquities."

the captain of the temple (4:1)—chief of the temple police force, and second in command to the High Priest

4:1 Now as they spoke to the people, the priests, the captain of the temple, and the Sadducees came upon them,

2 being greatly disturbed that they taught the people and preached in Jesus the resurrection from the dead.

already evening (v. 3)—Jewish law did not allow trials or hearings at night

3 And they laid hands on them, and put them in custody until the next day, for it was already evening.

five thousand (v. 4)—the total number of men in the Jerusalem church

4 However, many of those who heard the word believed; and the number of the men came to be about five thousand.

5 And it came to pass, on the next day, that their rulers, elders, and scribes,

6 *as well as Annas the high priest, Caiaphas, John, and Alexander, and as many as were of the family of the high priest, were gathered together at Jerusalem.*

7 *And when they had set them in the midst, they asked, "By what power or by what name have you done this?"*

8 *Then Peter, filled with the Holy Spirit, said to them, "Rulers of the people and elders of Israel:*

filled with the Holy Spirit (v. 8)—This explains Peter's eloquent and powerful preaching.

9 *If we this day are judged for a good deed done to a helpless man, by what means he has been made well,*

10 *let it be known to you all, and to all the people of Israel, that by the name of Jesus Christ of Nazareth, whom you crucified, whom God raised from the dead, by Him this man stands here before you whole.*

11 *This is the 'stone which was rejected by you builders, which has become the chief cornerstone.'*

12 *Nor is there salvation in any other, for there is no other name under heaven given among men by which we must be saved."*

no other name (v. 12)—There are only two religious paths: the broad (and futile) way of works to achieve salvation that ultimately leads to eternal death, and the narrow way of faith in Jesus, leading to eternal life.

13 *Now when they saw the boldness of Peter and John, and perceived that they were uneducated and untrained men, they marveled. And they realized that they had been with Jesus.*

14 *And seeing the man who had been healed standing with them, they could say nothing against it.*

15 *But when they had commanded them to go aside out of the council, they conferred among themselves,*

16 *saying, "What shall we do to these men? For, indeed, that a notable miracle has been done through them is evident to all who dwell in Jerusalem, and we cannot deny it.*

17 *But so that it spreads no further among the people, let us severely threaten them, that from now on they speak to no man in this name."*

18 *So they called them and commanded them not to speak at all nor teach in the name of Jesus.*

to listen to you more than to God (v. 19)—Christians should always obey governmental authority, unless that authority commands something contrary to God's Word.

Lord (v. 24)—a rare term that means "absolute master" and implies sovereignty

19 But Peter and John answered and said to them, "Whether it is right in the sight of God to listen to you more than to God, you judge.

20 For we cannot but speak the things which we have seen and heard."

21 So when they had further threatened them, they let them go, finding no way of punishing them, because of the people, since they all glorified God for what had been done.

22 For the man was over forty years old on whom this miracle of healing had been performed.

23 And being let go, they went to their own companions and reported all that the chief priests and elders had said to them.

24 So when they heard that, they raised their voice to God with one accord and said: "Lord, You are God, who made heaven and earth and the sea, and all that is in them,

25 who by the mouth of Your servant David have said: 'Why did the nations rage, And the people plot vain things?

26 The kings of the earth took their stand, And the rulers were gathered together Against the LORD and against His Christ.'

27 "For truly against Your holy Servant Jesus, whom You anointed, both Herod and Pontius Pilate, with the Gentiles and the people of Israel, were gathered together

28 to do whatever Your hand and Your purpose determined before to be done.

29 Now, Lord, look on their threats, and grant to Your servants that with all boldness they may speak Your word,

30 by stretching out Your hand to heal, and that signs and wonders may be done through the name of Your holy Servant Jesus."

31 And when they had prayed, the place where they were assembled together was shaken; and they were all filled with the Holy Spirit, and they spoke the word of God with boldness.

32 Now the multitude of those who believed were of one heart and one soul; neither did anyone say that any of the things he possessed was his own, but they had all things in common.

33 And with great power the apostles gave witness to the resurrection of the Lord Jesus. And great grace was upon them all.

34 Nor was there anyone among them who lacked; for all who were possessors of lands or houses sold them, and brought the proceeds of the things that were sold,

35 and laid them at the apostles' feet; and they distributed to each as anyone had need.

36 And Joses, who was also named Barnabas by the apostles (which is translated Son of Encouragement), a Levite of the country of Cyprus,

37 having land, sold it, and brought the money and laid it at the apostles' feet.

5:1 But a certain man named Ananias, with Sapphira his wife, sold a possession.

2 And he kept back part of the proceeds, his wife also being aware of it, and brought a certain part and laid it at the apostles' feet.

3 But Peter said, "Ananias, why has Satan filled your heart to lie to the Holy Spirit and keep back part of the price of the land for yourself?

4 While it remained, was it not your own? And after it was sold, was it not in your own control? Why have you conceived this thing in your heart? You have not lied to men but to God."

5 Then Ananias, hearing these words, fell down and breathed his last. So great fear came upon all those who heard these things.

6 And the young men arose and wrapped him up, carried him out, and buried him.

7 Now it was about three hours later when his wife came in, not knowing what had happened.

8 And Peter answered her, "Tell me whether you sold the land for so much?" She said, "Yes, for so much."

all things in common (vv. 32–35)—When people in the church had needs, those who could help did so by giving money or possessions to the apostles for distribution.

great grace (v. 33)—that is, "favor"

kept back part of the proceeds (5:2)—not a sin in and of itself; however, they had promised the full amount received to the Lord; they lied in trying to appear more generous than they were

great fear (v. 5)—afraid over the seriousness of hypocrisy and the prospect of divine judgment

test the Spirit of the Lord (v. 9)—to presume upon God's forbearance

test the Spirit of the Lord (v. 9)—to presume upon God's forbearance

none . . . dared join them (v. 13)—They respected Christ's followers, but feared the deadly potential of joining the church.

shadow of Peter (v. 15)—They truly thought he possessed healing power that could be transmitted even through his shadow; the Scripture never says this.

9 Then Peter said to her, "How is it that you have agreed together to test the Spirit of the Lord? Look, the feet of those who have buried your husband are at the door, and they will carry you out."

10 Then immediately she fell down at his feet and breathed her last. And the young men came in and found her dead, and carrying her out, buried her by her husband.

11 So great fear came upon all the church and upon all who heard these things.

12 And through the hands of the apostles many signs and wonders were done among the people. And they were all with one accord in Solomon's Porch.

13 Yet none of the rest dared join them, but the people esteemed them highly.

14 And believers were increasingly added to the Lord, multitudes of both men and women,

15 so that they brought the sick out into the streets and laid them on beds and couches, that at least the shadow of Peter passing by might fall on some of them.

16 Also a multitude gathered from the surrounding cities to Jerusalem, bringing sick people and those who were tormented by unclean spirits, and they were all healed.

17 Then the high priest rose up, and all those who were with him (which is the sect of the Sadducees), and they were filled with indignation,

18 and laid their hands on the apostles and put them in the common prison.

19 But at night an angel of the Lord opened the prison doors and brought them out, and said,

20 "Go, stand in the temple and speak to the people all the words of this life."

21 And when they heard that, they entered the temple early in the morning and taught. But the high priest and those with him came and called the council together, with all the elders of the children of Israel, and sent to the prison to have them brought.

22 *But when the officers came and did not find them in the prison, they returned and reported,*

23 *saying, "Indeed we found the prison shut securely, and the guards standing outside before the doors; but when we opened them, we found no one inside!"*

24 *Now when the high priest, the captain of the temple, and the chief priests heard these things, they wondered what the outcome would be.*

25 *So one came and told them, saying, "Look, the men whom you put in prison are standing in the temple and teaching the people!"*

26 *Then the captain went with the officers and brought them without violence, for they feared the people, lest they should be stoned.*

27 *And when they had brought them, they set them before the council. And the high priest asked them,*

28 *saying, "Did we not strictly command you not to teach in this name? And look, you have filled Jerusalem with your doctrine, and intend to bring this Man's blood on us!"*

doctrine (v. 28)—that is, the gospel of Jesus Christ

29 *But Peter and the other apostles answered and said: "We ought to obey God rather than men.*

30 *The God of our fathers raised up Jesus whom you murdered by hanging on a tree.*

31 *Him God has exalted to His right hand to be Prince and Savior, to give repentance to Israel and forgiveness of sins.*

32 *And we are His witnesses to these things, and so also is the Holy Spirit whom God has given to those who obey Him."*

33 *When they heard this, they were furious and plotted to kill them.*

34 *Then one in the council stood up, a Pharisee named Gamaliel, a teacher of the law held in respect by all the people, and commanded them to put the apostles outside for a little while.*

Gamaliel (v. 34)—the grandson of the revered rabbi Hillel, and most noted rabbi of his time

35 *And he said to them: "Men of Israel, take heed to yourselves what you intend to do regarding these men.*

36 *For some time ago Theudas rose up, claiming to be somebody. A number of men, about four hundred, joined him. He was slain, and all who obeyed him were scattered and came to nothing.*

37 *After this man, Judas of Galilee rose up in the days of the census, and drew away many people after him. He also perished, and all who obeyed him were dispersed.*

38 *And now I say to you, keep away from these men and let them alone; for if this plan or this work is of men, it will come to nothing;*

39 *but if it is of God, you cannot overthrow it—lest you even be found to fight against God."*

beaten them (v. 40)—an unjust flogging, probably thirty-nine lashes (see Deut. 25:3)

40 *And they agreed with him, and when they had called for the apostles and beaten them, they commanded that they should not speak in the name of Jesus, and let them go.*

41 *So they departed from the presence of the council, rejoicing that they were counted worthy to suffer shame for His name.*

42 *And daily in the temple, and in every house, they did not cease teaching and preaching Jesus as the Christ.*

1) How did the healing of the blind man at the temple promote the spread of the gospel?

_____

_____

_____

_____

2) List all the names for Jesus that Peter used in his preaching (3:12–26; 4:8–12; 5:29–31). How had the disciples' view of Jesus expanded?

_____

_____

_____

_____

3) Describe the inner workings of the fledgling church during this time of growth, persecution, and then divine judgment. What qualities stand out to you?

_____

_____

_____

Going Deeper

Later on, the apostle Paul helped to define more clearly what a leader in the church should look like. Read Titus 1:5–9.

Exploring the Meaning

4) Compare the requirements for church leaders that Paul gives in Titus with the leadership example set by the apostles in Acts 3–5.

_____

_____

_____

5) When is it acceptable (or even right) for a believer to disobey the civil authorities?

_____

_____

_____

(Verses to consider: Rom. 13:1–7; Dan. 6:4–10)

6) Acts 5:1–11 contains a sobering warning against sin in the church. Why do you think God's judgment came so swiftly on Ananias and Sapphira? What are the implications of this event for the church today?

_____

_____

_____

_____

(Verses to consider: Matt. 6:1–6, 16–18; 15:7; 23:23–36)

TRUTH FOR TODAY

Widespread confusion exists over what the primary mission of the church of Jesus Christ should be. Some argue that the church should lead the crusade for social justice for the poor and downtrodden. Others see it as a political force to help change the culture. Still others view their church as a private club, where they can socialize with their friends. On a more biblical note, the church's goal is to mature the saints through the preaching of the Word, fellowship, and discipleship. It also meets to praise and worship God. These are important goals that should mark every church. Yet none of them is the church's primary goal here on earth. Indeed, every one of them could be better accomplished in heaven.

What is the primary goal of the church? Our Lord answered that question by charging us to "Go therefore and make disciples of all the nations, baptizing them in the name of the Father and the Son and the Holy Spirit, teaching them to observe all things that I have commanded you" (Matt. 28:19–20 NKJV). The church's primary goal is evangelism. It is to carry on the work begun by the Lord Jesus Christ, whose mission was "to seek and to save that which was lost" (Luke 19:10 NKJV). That is the only duty of the church that can't be better done in heaven.

REFLECTING ON THE TEXT

7) In the face of persecution, the early church became even bolder in their witness. How do you account for that fact?

_____

_____

_____

_____

_____

8) Who have been the most effective spiritual leaders in your life? Why?

_____

_____

_____

_____

_____

9) What practical steps can you take to help make your local congregation more like the body of believers depicted here—in praying? In sharing? In modeling the gospel? In leading others to Christ? In purity?

_____

_____

_____

Personal Response

Write out additional reflections, questions you may have, or a prayer.

_____

_____

_____

_____

_____

_____

_____

_____

_____

_____

_____

_____

_____

_____

_____

_____

_____

_____

Additional Notes

3

THE DEACONS OF THE CHURCH

Acts 6:1–8:3

DRAWING NEAR

Many Christians unconsciously believe in an unwritten rule: "If I live a moral life and if I faithfully serve God, He is somewhat obligated to protect me from anything really bad." Do you agree with this rule? Why or why not?

_____

_____

_____

THE CONTEXT

The rapid growth of the first-century church meant an influx of people. More people meant more needs and new ministries to meet those needs. New programs meant administrative and logistical problems that threatened to consume all the apostles' time. Rather than neglect the spiritual disciplines of prayer and teaching God's Word, the apostles called and commissioned a group of men to attend to the pressing needs of the body.

Stephen was one of the church's newly appointed "deacons." With Christlike character, he ministered powerfully among the people until the day he encountered a group of argumentative Jews. After he declared the truth about God to them, they told lies about him to the Jewish authorities. For faithfully discharging his duties as a believer, Stephen was arrested! If Stephen was nervous as he stood before the high priest and powerful council of the Jews, he didn't show it. He gave the religious leaders a concise review of Jewish history and then abruptly accused the council of murdering the long-awaited Messiah. This blunt and pointed sermon sent the Jews into a rage and resulted in the first martyrdom in church history.

Stephen's death seemed to escalate the Jews' persecution of the followers of Christ. The man named Saul proved to be a major leader in this widespread campaign of intolerance and terror. From a human perspective, this was an awful turn of events; from a divine perspective, everything resulted in a far greater good. The Christians were forced to scatter to the surrounding regions of Judea and Samaria. As they did, the gospel began to be preached to Gentile audiences. Thus, in the midst of terrible persecution, the church actually grew!

KEYS TO THE TEXT

Moses and the Law: Moses was the greatest and most revered of all the Old Testament prophets. The Ten Commandments and all the laws and instructions recorded in Exodus through Deuteronomy made up the "law of Moses." It was this law that the Jewish religious leaders held above all others. Stephen recounts the Israelites' history, including Moses' prediction that another greater prophet would come—Jesus.

Stoning: The usual method of capital punishment in ancient Israel. People who broke specific statutes of the law of Moses were put to death by stoning. Stoning was usually carried out by the men of the community, upon the testimony of at least two witnesses, who would then cast the first stones (Deut. 17:5–7; John 8:7; Acts 7:58). Stoning usually took place outside the settlement or camp. Offenses punishable by stoning were certain cases of disobedience, child sacrifice, consultation with magicians, blasphemy, breaking the Sabbath, the worship of false gods, rebellion against parents, and adultery. (*Nelson's New Illustrated Bible Dictionary*)

UNLEASHING THE TEXT

Read 6:1–8:3, noting the key words and definitions next to the passage.

multiplying (v. 1)—By this point, the church may have numbered twenty thousand

Hebrews . . . Hellenists (v. 1)—The "Hebrews" were Jews from Palestine; the "Hellenists" were Jews from elsewhere in the Greek world.

serve tables (v. 2)—The word translated "tables" can refer to tables used in financial matters; whether the situation involved meals or money, the apostles did not want to neglect their top priorities.

seven men (v. 3)—a temporary solution to a pressing need, not an official "office" of deacons; that came later in the development of the church

laid hands on them (v. 6)—a symbolic act demonstrating affirmation, support, and identification

Acts 6:1–8:3 (NKJV)

1 Now in those days, when the number of the disciples was multiplying, there arose a complaint against the Hebrews by the Hellenists, because their widows were neglected in the daily distribution.

2 Then the twelve summoned the multitude of the disciples and said, "It is not desirable that we should leave the word of God and serve tables.

3 Therefore, brethren, seek out from among you seven men of good reputation, full of the Holy Spirit and wisdom, whom we may appoint over this business;

4 but we will give ourselves continually to prayer and to the ministry of the word."

5 And the saying pleased the whole multitude. And they chose Stephen, a man full of faith and the Holy Spirit, and Philip, Prochorus, Nicanor, Timon, Parmenas, and Nicolas, a proselyte from Antioch,

6 whom they set before the apostles; and when they had prayed, they laid hands on them.

7 Then the word of God spread, and the number of the disciples multiplied greatly in Jerusalem, and a great many of the priests were obedient to the faith.

8 And Stephen, full of faith and power, did great wonders and signs among the people.

9 Then there arose some from what is called the Synagogue of the Freedmen (Cyrenians, Alexandrians, and those from Cilicia and Asia), disputing with Stephen.

Synagogue of the Freedman (v. 9)—probably three separate synagogues comprised of the groups listed

10 And they were not able to resist the wisdom and the Spirit by which he spoke.

11 Then they secretly induced men to say, "We have heard him speak blasphemous words against Moses and God."

blasphemous words (v. 11)— Unable to prevail over Stephen in a formal debate, these Jews resorted to deceit.

12 And they stirred up the people, the elders, and the scribes; and they came upon him, seized him, and brought him to the council.

13 They also set up false witnesses who said, "This man does not cease to speak blasphemous words against this holy place and the law;

14 for we have heard him say that this Jesus of Nazareth will destroy this place and change the customs which Moses delivered to us."

15 And all who sat in the council, looking steadfastly at him, saw his face as the face of an angel.

face of an angel (v. 15)—pure, calm, unruffled composure reflecting the presence of God

7:1 Then the high priest said, "Are these things so?"

high priest (7:1)—probably Caiaphas

2 And he said, "Brethren and fathers, listen: The God of glory appeared to our father Abraham when he was in Mesopotamia, before he dwelt in Haran,

3 and said to him, 'Get out of your country and from your relatives, and come to a land that I will show you.'

4 Then he came out of the land of the Chaldeans and dwelt in Haran. And from there, when his father was dead, He moved him to this land in which you now dwell.

5 And God gave him no inheritance in it, not even enough to set his foot on. But even when Abraham had no child, He promised to give it to him for a possession, and to his descendants after him.

four hundred years (v. 6)—an
approximate figure; see Genesis
15:13–14

twelve patriarchs (v. 8)—the
twelve sons of Jacob, who became the heads of the twelve
tribes of Israel

6 *But God spoke in this way: that his descendants
would dwell in a foreign land, and that they would
bring them into bondage and oppress them four
hundred years.*

7 *'And the nation to whom they will be in bondage I
will judge,' said God, 'and after that they shall come
out and serve Me in this place.'*

8 *Then He gave him the covenant of circumcision;
and so Abraham begot Isaac and circumcised him
on the eighth day; and Isaac begot Jacob, and Jacob
begot the twelve patriarchs.*

9 *"And the patriarchs, becoming envious, sold Joseph
into Egypt. But God was with him*

10 *and delivered him out of all his troubles, and gave
him favor and wisdom in the presence of Pharaoh,
king of Egypt; and he made him governor over
Egypt and all his house.*

11 *Now a famine and great trouble came over all the
land of Egypt and Canaan, and our fathers found
no sustenance.*

12 *But when Jacob heard that there was grain in Egypt,
he sent out our fathers first.*

13 *And the second time Joseph was made known to his
brothers, and Joseph's family became known to the
Pharaoh.*

14 *Then Joseph sent and called his father Jacob and all
his relatives to him, seventy-five people.*

15 *So Jacob went down to Egypt; and he died, he and
our fathers.*

16 *And they were carried back to Shechem and laid in
the tomb that Abraham bought for a sum of money
from the sons of Hamor, the father of Shechem.*

17 *"But when the time of the promise drew near which
God had sworn to Abraham, the people grew and
multiplied in Egypt*

18 *till another king arose who did not know Joseph.*

19 *This man dealt treacherously with our people, and
oppressed our forefathers, making them expose their
babies, so that they might not live.*

expose their babies (v. 19)—
only the male children

20 *At this time Moses was born, and was well pleasing to God; and he was brought up in his father's house for three months.*

21 *But when he was set out, Pharaoh's daughter took him away and brought him up as her own son.*

22 *And Moses was learned in all the wisdom of the Egyptians, and was mighty in words and deeds.*

23 *"Now when he was forty years old, it came into his heart to visit his brethren, the children of Israel.*

24 *And seeing one of them suffer wrong, he defended and avenged him who was oppressed, and struck down the Egyptian.*

25 *For he supposed that his brethren would have understood that God would deliver them by his hand, but they did not understand.*

26 *And the next day he appeared to two of them as they were fighting, and tried to reconcile them, saying, 'Men, you are brethren; why do you wrong one another?'*

27 *But he who did his neighbor wrong pushed him away, saying, 'Who made you a ruler and a judge over us?*

28 *Do you want to kill me as you did the Egyptian yesterday?'*

29 *Then, at this saying, Moses fled and became a dweller in the land of Midian, where he had two sons.*

30 *"And when forty years had passed, an Angel of the Lord appeared to him in a flame of fire in a bush, in the wilderness of Mount Sinai.*

31 *When Moses saw it, he marveled at the sight; and as he drew near to observe, the voice of the Lord came to him,*

32 *saying, 'I am the God of your fathers—the God of Abraham, the God of Isaac, and the God of Jacob.' And Moses trembled and dared not look.*

33 *'Then the LORD said to him, "Take your sandals off your feet, for the place where you stand is holy ground.*

34 *I have surely seen the oppression of My people who are in Egypt; I have heard their groaning and have*

he was forty years old (v. 23)— Moses spent forty years in Pharaoh's court, forty years in exile in Midian, and forty years leading the Exodus and Israel's wilderness wanderings.

come down to deliver them. And now come, I will send you to Egypt." '

35 "This Moses whom they rejected, saying, 'Who made you a ruler and a judge?' is the one God sent to be a ruler and a deliverer by the hand of the Angel who appeared to him in the bush.

36 He brought them out, after he had shown wonders and signs in the land of Egypt, and in the Red Sea, and in the wilderness forty years.

37 "This is that Moses who said to the children of Israel, 'The LORD your God will raise up for you a Prophet like me from your brethren. Him you shall hear.'

38 "This is he who was in the congregation in the wilderness with the Angel who spoke to him on Mount Sinai, and with our fathers, the one who received the living oracles to give to us,

would not obey (v. 39)—Israel would not follow Moses' leadership and yearned to return to slavery in Egypt.

39 whom our fathers would not obey, but rejected. And in their hearts they turned back to Egypt,

40 saying to Aaron, 'Make us gods to go before us; as for this Moses who brought us out of the land of Egypt, we do not know what has become of him.'

41 And they made a calf in those days, offered sacrifices to the idol, and rejoiced in the works of their own hands.

God . . . gave them up to worship the host of heaven (v. 42)—God abandoned the people to their sin of idolatry.

42 Then God turned and gave them up to worship the host of heaven, as it is written in the book of the Prophets: 'Did you offer Me slaughtered animals and sacrifices during forty years in the wilderness, O house of Israel?

43 You also took up the tabernacle of Moloch, And the star of your god Remphan, Images which you made to worship; And I will carry you away beyond Babylon.'

tabernacle of witness (v. 44)—the predecessor of the temple

44 "Our fathers had the tabernacle of witness in the wilderness, as He appointed, instructing Moses to make it according to the pattern that he had seen,

45 which our fathers, having received it in turn, also brought with Joshua into the land possessed by the Gentiles, whom God drove out before the face of our fathers until the days of David,

46 who found favor before God and asked to find a dwelling for the God of Jacob.

47 But Solomon built Him a house.

48 "However, the Most High does not dwell in temples made with hands, as the prophet says:

49 'Heaven is My throne, And earth is My footstool. What house will you build for Me? says the LORD, Or what is the place of My rest?

50 Has My hand not made all these things?'

51 "You stiff-necked and uncircumcised in heart and ears! You always resist the Holy Spirit; as your fathers did, so do you.

52 Which of the prophets did your fathers not persecute? And they killed those who foretold the coming of the Just One, of whom you now have become the betrayers and murderers,

53 who have received the law by the direction of angels and have not kept it."

54 When they heard these things they were cut to the heart, and they gnashed at him with their teeth.

55 But he, being full of the Holy Spirit, gazed into heaven and saw the glory of God, and Jesus standing at the right hand of God,

56 and said, "Look! I see the heavens opened and the Son of Man standing at the right hand of God!"

57 Then they cried out with a loud voice, stopped their ears, and ran at him with one accord;

58 and they cast him out of the city and stoned him. And the witnesses laid down their clothes at the feet of a young man named Saul.

59 And they stoned Stephen as he was calling on God and saying, "Lord Jesus, receive my spirit."

60 Then he knelt down and cried out with a loud voice, "Lord, do not charge them with this sin." And when he had said this, he fell asleep.

8:1 Now Saul was consenting to his death. At that time a great persecution arose against the church which was at Jerusalem; and they were all scattered throughout the regions of Judea and Samaria, except the apostles.

stiff-necked (v. 51)—obstinate, like their forefathers

uncircumcised in heart and ears! (v. 51)—thus, as unclean before God as the uncircumcised Gentiles

resist the Holy Spirit (v. 51)—by rejecting the Spirit's messengers and their message

gnashed . . . with their teeth (v. 54)—in anger and frustration

laid down their clothes . . . Saul (v. 58)—Paul's first appearance in Scripture reveals him to be deeply involved in this sordid, murderous scene.

stoned (v. 59)—the legal punishment for blasphemy; however, this was not a legal execution but an act of mob violence

do not charge them with this sin (v. 60)—a Christlike plea for his killers' forgiveness

he fell asleep (v. 60)—a common New Testament euphemism for the death of believers

scattered (8:1)—Thus began a widespread persecution of Christians that caused many to flee Jerusalem.

made havoc (v. 3)—a verb used in extrabiblical Greek writings to refer to the destruction of a city or mangling by a wild animal

2 And devout men carried Stephen to his burial, and made great lamentation over him.

3 As for Saul, he made havoc of the church, entering every house, and dragging off men and women, committing them to prison.

1) What situation prompted the leaders of the early church to take steps to organize more efficiently, appointing Stephen and others to special positions of service?

_____

_____

_____

2) Consider this statement: "We dare not try to force the Spirit to fit our mold. Organization is never an end itself but only a means to facilitate what the Lord is already doing in His church." Do you agree or disagree with this statement? Why?

_____

_____

_____

3) What were the requirements for the men chosen to lead the church in serving ministries? Why would these qualities be needed?

_____

_____

_____

4) How would you characterize Stephen's message to the Jews? Was it "seeker sensitive"? Was it hotheaded? Misguided? What were Stephen's major points?

_____

_____

_____

GOING DEEPER

In some ways, the Old Testament prophet Jeremiah's task was similar to Stephen's situation. Read Jeremiah 7:23–28.

Exploring the Meaning

5) What did God say the results would be when Jeremiah faithfully proclaimed the truth of God to the people of Israel?

_____

_____

6) What implications does this hold for modern-day Christians called to share the truth of the gospel with a secular culture?

_____

_____

7) What happened immediately following Stephen's death? Why do you think his murder did not placate those who were opposed to the gospel?

_____

_____

_____

Truth for Today

At first glance, Stephen's death may seem pointless. Here was a promising career cut short. His ministry seems to have ended in failure. Not only was he killed as a heretic, but his death also triggered the first persecution against the entire church. That persecution, spearheaded by Saul of Tarsus, scattered the Jerusalem fellowship. Such a skewed view of Stephen's death, however, betrays a lack of understanding of the way the Holy Spirit works. The persecution, which seemed to be a negative, was in reality a positive factor. It led to the first great missionary outreach by the early church. Satan's attempt to stamp out the church's fire merely scattered the embers and started new fires around the world. In the words of the early church Father Tertullian, the blood of the martyrs became the seed of the church.

Reflecting on the Text

8) Review the description of the deacons in 6:3–5. If you had been in the early church, what personal character flaws might have disqualified you from a position of service? In what areas do you need to grow?

_____

_____

9) Stephen's presentation of the gospel to the Jews might be labeled bold, even blunt. When is it appropriate to speak hard words to the lost and to be more confrontational regarding sin? Who in your life might benefit from such tough love?

_____

_____

_____

10) Today, persecution of believers is happening around the world. Some 200 million Christians (your brothers and sisters in the faith!) face ongoing suffering, torture, and even death simply because of their commitment to Jesus Christ. What can you do for them? How can you encourage them?

_____

_____

_____

11) How would you answer the person who said: "I don't see any way that any good can possibly come from the suffering and persecution of Christians"?

_____

_____

_____

PERSONAL RESPONSE

Write out additional reflections, questions you may have, or a prayer.

_____

_____

_____

_____

_____

_____

_____

4

The Gospel Begins to Spread Beyond Jerusalem

Drawing Near

As the church grew, the believers had to depend on God's Spirit more than ever for direction and wisdom. Think of a time when you knew with certainty that God was leading you to do something. How did you know? What happened?

_____

_____

_____

_____

The Context

Acts 1:8 is one of the most significant verses in the entire book. It not only serves as a blueprint for God's global plan but also functions as a kind of outline for Luke's inspired record. Chapters 1–7 detail the action of Christ's witnesses in Jerusalem. Beginning with the persecution led by Saul in chapter 8, the gospel began to spread as Christ had commanded.

Luke recorded Philip's trip into Samaria and his ministry there in order to reveal the marvelous truth that Jesus, the promised Jewish Messiah, was also the King and Savior of Gentiles. The message of Christ was and is a *worldwide* gospel. All nations and languages would be invited and included in the kingdom of God (see Isa. 56:3; Dan. 7:14). Philip was sovereignly instructed to suddenly leave a booming ministry in Samaria to go south into the desert. There he met a prominent official from the court of Candace, the queen of Ethiopia, reading (but not understanding) the prophet Isaiah. The succeeding story of Philip and the Ethiopian eunuch provides a wonderful picture of God's global love and His surprising plan to get the good news of Christ to those who have never heard. Even though there is opposition, the underlying truth of this section of Acts is clear: Nothing can stop God's powerful and eternal plan to fill heaven with worshipers from "every nation and tribe and people and language" (Rev. 7:9 NKJV).

KEYS TO THE TEXT

The City of Samaria. The ancient capital of the northern kingdom of Israel, which eventually fell to the Assyrians (722 BC after over 200 years of idolatry and rebellion against God). After resettling many of the people in other lands, the Assyrians located Gentiles from other areas into the region, resulting in a mix of Jews and Gentiles who became known as Samaritans. The Samaritans withdrew from the worship of Yahweh at Jerusalem and established their worship at Mount Gerizim in Samaria. As a result of this history, Jews repudiated Samaritans and considered them heretical. Intense ethnic and cultural tensions raged historically between the two groups so that both avoided contact as much as possible.

Miracles, Wonders, and Signs: Many miracles accompanied the spread of the good news. "Wonders" refers to the amazement people experience when witnessing supernatural miracles. "Signs" point to the power of God behind miracles. Marvels have no value unless they point to God and His truth. Throughout the book of Acts such works were often done by the Holy Spirit through the apostles and their associates to authenticate them as the messengers of God's truth.

UNLEASHING THE TEXT

Read 8:4–40, noting the key words and definitions next to the passage.

Acts 8:4–40 (NKJV)

went everywhere (v. 4)—a common expression in Acts for missionary efforts

Philip (v. 5)—the first missionary named in Scripture and the first person to be given the title "evangelist"

Samaria (v. 5)—the ancient capital of the northern kingdom of Israel; the inhabitants at the time (that is, the Samaritans) had a mixed ancestry, creating cultural and racial barriers between them and the pure-blooded Jews

sorcery (v. 9)—magic which originally referred to the Medo-Persians; a mixture of science and superstition, including astrology, divination, and the occult

4 *Therefore those who were scattered went everywhere preaching the word.*

5 *Then Philip went down to the city of Samaria and preached Christ to them.*

6 *And the multitudes with one accord heeded the things spoken by Philip, hearing and seeing the miracles which he did.*

7 *For unclean spirits, crying with a loud voice, came out of many who were possessed; and many who were paralyzed and lame were healed.*

8 *And there was great joy in that city.*

9 *But there was a certain man called Simon, who previously practiced sorcery in the city and astonished the people of Samaria, claiming that he was someone great,*

10 *to whom they all gave heed, from the least to the*

greatest, saying, "This man is the great power of God."

11 And they heeded him because he had astonished them with his sorceries for a long time.

12 But when they believed Philip as he preached the things concerning the kingdom of God and the name of Jesus Christ, both men and women were baptized.

13 Then Simon himself also believed; and when he was baptized he continued with Philip, and was amazed, seeing the miracles and signs which were done.

14 Now when the apostles who were at Jerusalem heard that Samaria had received the word of God, they sent Peter and John to them,

15 who, when they had come down, prayed for them that they might receive the Holy Spirit.

16 For as yet He had fallen upon none of them. They had only been baptized in the name of the Lord Jesus.

17 Then they laid hands on them, and they received the Holy Spirit.

18 And when Simon saw that through the laying on of the apostles' hands the Holy Spirit was given, he offered them money,

19 saying, "Give me this power also, that anyone on whom I lay hands may receive the Holy Spirit."

20 But Peter said to him, "Your money perish with you, because you thought that the gift of God could be purchased with money!

21 You have neither part nor portion in this matter, for your heart is not right in the sight of God.

22 Repent therefore of this your wickedness, and pray God if perhaps the thought of your heart may be forgiven you.

23 For I see that you are poisoned by bitterness and bound by iniquity."

24 Then Simon answered and said, "Pray to the Lord for me, that none of the things which you have spoken may come upon me."

"This man is the great power of God." (v. 10)—a claim to be united with God

Simon . . . believed . . . was baptized (v. 13)—As the narrative indicates, Simon's belief was motivated by purely selfish reasons and was not genuine faith.

as yet . . . upon none of them (v. 16)—Used by some to argue that Christians receive the Holy Spirit subsequent to salvation, this view fails to take into account the fact that these incidents took place during a transitional period in church history in which confirmation by the apostles was necessary to verify inclusion of a new group of people into the church (in this instance, nothing less than a divine sign would convince Jewish believers that the detested Samaritans were also part of God's plan for the church).

laid hands on them (v. 17)—indicating apostolic authority and confirmation

received the Holy Spirit (v. 17)—likely a replication of the events from Pentecost (that is, speaking in tongues) in order to show unmistakably that the way of salvation was open to the Gentiles as well as to the Jews

Gaza (v. 26)—one of the five cities of the Philistines

eunuch (v. 27)—This term can refer either to one who had been emasculated or, in more general terms, to a government official. He may have functioned as a kind of Treasury Secretary or Minister of Finance for Candace, the queen mother of Ethiopia.

The place . . . he read (v. 32)—Isaiah 53:7–8

of whom does the prophet say this . . . ? (v. 34)—The man's confusion was understandable; even the Jewish rabbis argued about the interpretation of this passage.

25 So when they had testified and preached the word of the Lord, they returned to Jerusalem, preaching the gospel in many villages of the Samaritans.

26 Now an angel of the Lord spoke to Philip, saying, "Arise and go toward the south along the road which goes down from Jerusalem to Gaza." This is desert.

27 So he arose and went. And behold, a man of Ethiopia, a eunuch of great authority under Candace the queen of the Ethiopians, who had charge of all her treasury, and had come to Jerusalem to worship,

28 was returning. And sitting in his chariot, he was reading Isaiah the prophet.

29 Then the Spirit said to Philip, "Go near and overtake this chariot."

30 So Philip ran to him, and heard him reading the prophet Isaiah, and said, "Do you understand what you are reading?"

31 And he said, "How can I, unless someone guides me?" And he asked Philip to come up and sit with him.

32 The place in the Scripture which he read was this: "He was led as a sheep to the slaughter; And as a lamb before its shearer is silent, So He opened not His mouth.

33 In His humiliation His justice was taken away, And who will declare His generation? For His life is taken from the earth."

34 So the eunuch answered Philip and said, "I ask you, of whom does the prophet say this, of himself or of some other man?"

35 Then Philip opened his mouth, and beginning at this Scripture, preached Jesus to him.

36 Now as they went down the road, they came to some water. And the eunuch said, "See, here is water. What hinders me from being baptized?"

37 Then Philip said, "If you believe with all your heart, you may." And he answered and said, "I believe that Jesus Christ is the Son of God."

38 *So he commanded the chariot to stand still. And both Philip and the eunuch went down into the water, and he baptized him.*

39 *Now when they came up out of the water, the Spirit of the Lord caught Philip away, so that the eunuch saw him no more; and he went on his way rejoicing.*

40 *But Philip was found at Azotus. And passing through, he preached in all the cities till he came to Caesarea.*

caught Philip away (v. 39)—snatched away in miraculous fashion, just as Elijah and Ezekiel had been in the Old Testament

1) What does it mean that the believers "went everywhere" preaching the word?

_____

_____

_____

(Verses to consider: Acts 9:32; 13:6; 14:24; 15:3, 41; 16:6; 18:23; 19:1, 21; 20:2)

2) Based on the record of chapter 8, was Simon a true Christian or not? Explain your answer.

_____

_____

_____

3) How did Philip's encounter with the Ethiopian eunuch come about?

_____

_____

_____

4) How do you see the Spirit's continuing role in the growth of the church?

_____

_____

_____

Going Deeper

Read Matthew 13:1–23 for more insight about sharing God's Word.

Exploring the Meaning

5) How does the parable of the soils in Matthew 13 illustrate the varying reactions to the gospel that are reported in Acts 8?

Simon – rocks – didn't really understand what was committing to

Eunich – good soil

6) What events in chapter 8 suggest satanic opposition to the spread of the gospel? In other words, what demonic and worldly roadblocks did the believers encounter as they took the gospel into Samaritan territory?

Simon the Sorcerer

7) Some Christians point to chapter 8 as proof that believers need to seek a "second blessing." By this they mean that believers need to be baptized in the Holy Spirit at some point following salvation. What evidence do you see for this? Against this?

(Verses to consider: Rom. 8:9; 1 Cor. 12:13)

Truth for Today

God often accomplishes His sovereign work through human instruments (see 2:4, 14; 4:8, 31; 6:3–8; 7:55; 8:17; 10:1–48; 16:25–34). Like a master sculptor, He takes otherwise useless and inconsequential tools and uses them to create a masterpiece. There is a prerequisite, however, for being used by God. Paul writes, "Now in a large house there are not only gold and silver vessels, but also vessels of wood and of earthenware, and some to honor and some to dishonor. Therefore, if a man cleanses himself from these things, he will be a vessel for honor, sanctified, useful to the Master, prepared for every good work" (2 Tim. 2:20–21 NKJV). God uses holy tools to do His work.

REFLECTING ON THE TEXT

8) Simon tried to be used by God, but failed. How is Simon's story a sober warning to all in the church who claim to be believers in Christ?

_____

_____

_____

_____

9) Why do you think God called Philip away from a thriving ministry to many and sent him to speak to one solitary individual in the desert? What are the implications of this divine act for your own life?

_____

_____

_____

10) As a child of God who has been commanded to make disciples of all nations, how specifically do you sense God is leading you to share the gospel this week? What can you do to become a more effective witness?

_____

_____

_____

_____

PERSONAL RESPONSE

Write out additional reflections, questions you may have, or a prayer.

Prayer for Ben's Thailand Vietnam flight missions
Kai-ya's parents going to OR
Rachel - going to wedding

_____

_____

ADDITIONAL NOTES

~5~
THE CONVERSION OF SAUL

Acts 9:1–31

DRAWING NEAR

What is your conversion story? How did you come to believe in Christ? What was your life like before? In what tangible ways has Jesus Christ transformed you?

_____

_____

_____

_____

THE CONTEXT

As our study continues into chapter 9, Luke records a monumental event in the history of the church—the conversion of Saul of Tarsus. It was Saul (Paul) who would become God's apostle to the Gentiles, leading the church in spreading Christianity "to the ends of the earth." Therefore it is Paul, more than any other person, who figures prominently in Acts 10 through 28. No one else was better suited to the task than Paul: a "Hebrew of the Hebrews" (Phil. 3:5; Gal. 1:14); a native of Tarsus, thus thoroughly acquainted with Greek culture (17:22–31); a citizen of Rome (16:37); trained in a trade so that he could support himself (18:3) as he traveled and ministered.

But before Christ could use this highly gifted man, He first had to transform him. And thus we have the record of his life-changing encounter with Christ on the Damascus road! The change in Saul was instantaneous. In less than one week he went from "breathing threats and murder against the disciples of the Lord" (9:1) to "[preaching] the Christ in the synagogues, that He is the Son of God" (9:20).

The church was understandably suspicious, but Saul's powerful and persistent preaching, coupled with efforts by the Jewish authorities to kill him, finally convinced the apostles that Saul's conversion was genuine. According to Galatians 1:17–18, Saul/Paul spent about three years in Arabia between the time of his conversion and his journey to Jerusalem. According to Luke, following Saul's acceptance by the apostles, the church enjoyed another growth spurt and a time of peace.

45

KEYS TO THE TEXT

Saul/Paul: Like his namesake, Saul, Israel's first king, Paul was from the tribe of Benjamin. (*Saul* was his Hebrew name; *Paul* his Greek name). He was also a Roman citizen. Paul was born about the time of Christ's birth, in Tarsus, an important city in the Roman province of Cilicia, located in Asia Minor (modern Turkey). He spent much of his early life in Jerusalem as a student of the celebrated rabbi Gamaliel. Like his father before him, Paul was a Pharisee, a member of the strictest Jewish sect. Miraculously converted while on his way to Damascus (ca. AD 33–34) to arrest Christians in that city, Paul immediately began proclaiming the gospel message. Paul received the Spirit without any apostles present because he was a Jew (the inclusion of Jews in the church had already been established at Pentecost), and because he was an apostle in his own right, since Christ personally chose him and commissioned him for service. After narrowly escaping from Damascus with his life, Paul spent three years in Nabatean Arabia, south and east of the Dead Sea (Gal. 1:17, 18). During that time, he received much of his doctrine as direct revelation from the Lord. More than any other individual, Paul was responsible for the spread of Christianity throughout the Roman Empire.

UNLEASHING THE TEXT

Read 9:1–31, noting the key words and definitions next to the passage.

threats and murder (v. 1)—Saul was not a benign or passive opponent of the gospel, but a bitter enemy.

Damascus (v. 2)—The capital of Syria, some sixty miles inland from the Mediterranean and 160 miles northeast of Jerusalem; apparently a large number of Jews had fled there to escape the persecution mentioned in 8:2.

the Way (v. 2)—a designation for Christianity from Jesus' description of Himself in John 14:6; used in Acts frequently (19:9, 23; 22:4; 24:14, 22)

a light shone around him (v. 3)—the first of six visions of Paul recorded in Acts (16:9; 18:9; 22:17; 23:11; 27:23); this was an appearance of Jesus Christ in glory, visible only to Saul

Acts 9:1–31 (NKJV)

1 *Then Saul, still breathing threats and murder against the disciples of the Lord, went to the high priest*

2 *and asked letters from him to the synagogues of Damascus, so that if he found any who were of the Way, whether men or women, he might bring them bound to Jerusalem.*

3 *As he journeyed he came near Damascus, and suddenly a light shone around him from heaven.*

4 *Then he fell to the ground, and heard a voice saying to him, "Saul, Saul, why are you persecuting Me?"*

5 *And he said, "Who are You, Lord?" Then the Lord said, "I am Jesus, whom you are persecuting. It is hard for you to kick against the goads."*

6 *So he, trembling and astonished, said, "Lord, what do You want me to do?" Then the Lord said to him,*

"Arise and go into the city, and you will be told what you must do."

7 And the men who journeyed with him stood speechless, hearing a voice but seeing no one.

8 Then Saul arose from the ground, and when his eyes were opened he saw no one. But they led him by the hand and brought him into Damascus.

9 And he was three days without sight, and neither ate nor drank.

10 Now there was a certain disciple at Damascus named Ananias; and to him the Lord said in a vision, "Ananias." And he said, "Here I am, Lord."

11 So the Lord said to him, "Arise and go to the street called Straight, and inquire at the house of Judas for one called Saul of Tarsus, for behold, he is praying.

12 And in a vision he has seen a man named Ananias coming in and putting his hand on him, so that he might receive his sight."

13 Then Ananias answered, "Lord, I have heard from many about this man, how much harm he has done to Your saints in Jerusalem.

14 And here he has authority from the chief priests to bind all who call on Your name."

15 But the Lord said to him, "Go, for he is a chosen vessel of Mine to bear My name before Gentiles, kings, and the children of Israel.

16 For I will show him how many things he must suffer for My name's sake."

17 And Ananias went his way and entered the house; and laying his hands on him he said, "Brother Saul, the Lord Jesus, who appeared to you on the road as you came, has sent me that you may receive your sight and be filled with the Holy Spirit."

18 Immediately there fell from his eyes something like scales, and he received his sight at once; and he arose and was baptized.

19 So when he had received food, he was strengthened. Then Saul spent some days with the disciples at Damascus.

why are you persecuting Me? (v. 4)—Saul's persecution of Christians was tantamount to a direct attack on Christ.

goads (v. 5)—sticks for prodding cattle

Ananias (v. 10)—one of the leaders of the Damascus church and thus one of Saul's targets

Tarsus (v. 11)—birthplace of Saul; a key commercial and educational center near the border of Asia Minor and Syria

chosen vessel (v. 15)—literally, "a vessel of election"; God selected Paul to convey His grace to all men

be filled with the Holy Spirit (v. 17)—Saul was empowered for service; he received the Spirit without any apostles being present because Christ personally chose him and because he was a Jew (and the inclusion of Jews in the church had already been established at Pentecost).

He is the Son of God. (v. 20) —the content of Paul's lifelong message

after many days were past (v. 23)—Galatians 1:17–18 gives this number as three years, during which time Paul ministered in Nabatean Arabia.

gates (v. 24)—Damascus was a walled city, thus the gates were the only conventional avenue of escape.

a large basket (v. 25)—a woven hamper suitable for hay, straw, or bales of wool

Hellenists (v. 29)—the same group Stephen debated

Caesarea (v. 30)—an important port city on the Mediterranean, located thirty miles north of Joppa; the capital of the Roman province of Judea, home of the Roman procurator; site of the headquarters for a large Roman garrison

sent him out to Tarsus (v. 30)—Paul stepped out of the limelight, in all likelihood to ponder, reflect, and prepare for a later public, worldwide mission; he may have founded some churches around Syria and Cilicia during this time (15:23; Gal.1:21).

the churches . . . had peace and were edified. (v. 31)—Paul's conversion contributed to this time of tranquility.

20 Immediately he preached the Christ in the synagogues, that He is the Son of God.

21 Then all who heard were amazed, and said, "Is this not he who destroyed those who called on this name in Jerusalem, and has come here for that purpose, so that he might bring them bound to the chief priests?"

22 But Saul increased all the more in strength, and confounded the Jews who dwelt in Damascus, proving that this Jesus is the Christ.

23 Now after many days were past, the Jews plotted to kill him.

24 But their plot became known to Saul. And they watched the gates day and night, to kill him.

25 Then the disciples took him by night and let him down through the wall in a large basket.

26 And when Saul had come to Jerusalem, he tried to join the disciples; but they were all afraid of him, and did not believe that he was a disciple.

27 But Barnabas took him and brought him to the apostles. And he declared to them how he had seen the Lord on the road, and that He had spoken to him, and how he had preached boldly at Damascus in the name of Jesus.

28 So he was with them at Jerusalem, coming in and going out.

29 And he spoke boldly in the name of the Lord Jesus and disputed against the Hellenists, but they attempted to kill him.

30 When the brethren found out, they brought him down to Caesarea and sent him out to Tarsus.

31 Then the churches throughout all Judea, Galilee, and Samaria had peace and were edified. And walking in the fear of the Lord and in the comfort of the Holy Spirit, they were multiplied.

1) What happened to Saul as he made his way to Damascus to round up more Christians?

_____

_____

_____

(Verses to consider: Acts 22:14; 26:16; 1 Cor. 9:1; 15:8)

2) How did his traveling companions react?

_____

_____

3) What specifically did God ask Ananias to do, and why was this a troubling command?

_____

_____

_____

4) What was the ironic twist in Saul's story (9:2, 23, 29)?

_____

_____

_____

5) Acts records that Christianity was often referred to as "the Way" in the first century (see 9:2; 19:9, 23; 22:4; 24:14, 22). What does this mean?

_____

_____

_____

(Verses to consider: 18:26; John 14:6; Heb. 10:19–20; 2 Pet. 2:2)

GOING DEEPER

Read Philippians 3:1–14 for more insight into Paul's thinking about his relationship with Christ.

EXPLORING THE MEANING

6) How does Paul compare and contrast his life before and after meeting Christ?

Righteousness thru faith in Christ

7) Read Romans 3. Consider the way in which Paul met Christ. Is salvation initiated by God or by humanity? What are the implications of this for your prayer life?

8) What kinds of thoughts and feelings do you imagine Paul experienced during the three days he was without sight, while he fasted and waited for divine instructions (9:6–9)?

3 Day Story Inter - Varsity

TRUTH FOR TODAY

The Spirit transformed Saul in two fundamental ways. First, He took Saul's natural strengths and refined them. Saul was a gifted natural leader, with strong will power. He was a man of strong convictions, a self-starter, bold, a master at using his time and talents, a motivated individual, and a profoundly gifted thinker and speaker. The Holy Spirit also eliminated undesirable characteristics and replaced them with desirable ones. He replaced Paul's cruel hatred with love; his restless, aggressive spirit with peace; his rough, hard-nosed treatment of people with gentleness; his pride with humility. Only the Spirit of God can so thoroughly sanctify a life.

Reflecting on the Text

9) What natural strengths does God want to strengthen and use in your life? What undesirable qualities do you think the Lord wants to replace? What is necessary on your part for this process of sanctification to proceed?

_____

_____

_____

10) When has God used you to play an "Ananias" role in someone's life? What was that like?

_____

_____

_____

11) Write down the names of several people you know (or know of) who are highly antagonistic to the gospel. Begin to pray for them faithfully. Watch what God will do!

_____

_____

_____

Personal Response

Write out additional reflections, questions you may have, or a prayer.

_____

_____

_____

_____

_____

_____

_____

_____

ADDITIONAL NOTES

6

THE GOSPEL TO THE GENTILES

DRAWING NEAR

Someone has observed that in North America, Sunday morning seems to be the most segregated period of the whole week. Do you think this is an accurate observation? If so, what are the reasons for this reluctance of the church to transcend racial and cultural boundaries?

_____

_____

_____

When have you experienced a culturally diverse worship service? What did you appreciate about it?

_____

_____

_____

THE CONTEXT

After describing Saul's astounding conversion, Luke turned again to the ministry of Peter. In the first nine chapters, the convicting and regenerating work of God's Spirit has been mostly confined to the Jews. Beginning in chapter 10, Luke describes the Holy Spirit's sovereign activity in a Gentile army officer stationed on the Mediterranean coast. This is a watershed moment in the history of the church. The one true God—the God of the Hebrews—is about to unveil His eternal plan for the Gentiles.

To confirm the Gentiles' acceptance by God and their full inclusion in His kingdom as heirs of grace, Luke records the new converts' experience of the Holy Spirit. Exactly as happened with the Jewish believers at Pentecost, these new Gentile converts began speaking in unlearned foreign languages. The Jewish believers who had accompanied Peter from Joppa were amazed. To show that Peter's evangelistic encounter with the Gentile Cornelius was not a fluke, Luke mentions the widespread outreach that had begun taking place in Antioch. This effort to preach to non-Jews by believers from Cyprus and Cyrene had both the power and blessing of God on it.

Unable to stop the masses from embracing this new faith, the Jews launched a direct attack upon the leaders of the Christians. No more mere threats and warnings—this time, Herod had James executed and Peter arrested. Though from a human perspective the situation appeared terribly grim, from a heavenly perspective this was just another occasion to display the infinite power of God.

KEYS TO THE TEXT

Salvation to the Gentiles: Although the widespread salvation of Gentiles came about because Israel as a nation refused her Savior, that extension of grace was not an afterthought with God. From His first calling of Abraham, it was God's intent that His chosen people should be the instruments of bringing salvation to the Gentiles. "In you," the Lord told Abraham, "all the families of the earth shall be blessed" (Gen. 12:3 NKJV). In the covenant at Sinai God called Israel to be His witnesses, His spiritual ambassadors to the world as "a kingdom of priests and a holy nation" (Exod. 19:6 NKJV). The tribes of Jacob were to be "a light of the nations so that [God's] salvation may reach to the end of the earth" (Isa. 49:6 NKJV). God's ultimate plan of redemption has always included the Gentiles in every way as much as the Jews, His specially chosen people under the old covenant. Through Jesus Christ, believing Gentiles are as fully saved, as fully the children of God, and as fully citizens of His divine kingdom as are believing Jews. The church is the new people of God, called from among all nations.

UNLEASHING THE TEXT

Read 9:32–12:25, noting the key words and definitions next to the passage.

Acts 9:32–12:25 (NKJV)

32 Now it came to pass, as Peter went through all parts of the country, that he also came down to the saints who dwelt in Lydda.

33 There he found a certain man named Aeneas, who had been bedridden eight years and was paralyzed.

certain man (v. 33)—Aeneas was likely an unbeliever (see the phrase "certain disciple" in verse 36).

34 And Peter said to him, "Aeneas, Jesus the Christ heals you. Arise and make your bed." Then he arose immediately.

35 So all who dwelt at Lydda and Sharon saw him and turned to the Lord.

36 At Joppa there was a certain disciple named Tabitha, which is translated Dorcas. This woman

was full of good works and charitable deeds which she did.

37 But it happened in those days that she became sick and died. When they had washed her, they laid her in an upper room.

38 And since Lydda was near Joppa, and the disciples had heard that Peter was there, they sent two men to him, imploring him not to delay in coming to them.

39 Then Peter arose and went with them. When he had come, they brought him to the upper room. And all the widows stood by him weeping, showing the tunics and garments which Dorcas had made while she was with them.

40 But Peter put them all out, and knelt down and prayed. And turning to the body he said, "Tabitha, arise." And she opened her eyes, and when she saw Peter she sat up.

41 Then he gave her his hand and lifted her up; and when he had called the saints and widows, he presented her alive.

42 And it became known throughout all Joppa, and many believed on the Lord.

43 So it was that he stayed many days in Joppa with Simon, a tanner.

10:1 There was a certain man in Caesarea called Cornelius, a centurion of what was called the Italian Regiment,

2 a devout man and one who feared God with all his household, who gave alms generously to the people, and prayed to God always.

3 About the ninth hour of the day he saw clearly in a vision an angel of God coming in and saying to him, "Cornelius!"

4 And when he observed him, he was afraid, and said, "What is it, lord?" So he said to him, "Your prayers and your alms have come up for a memorial before God.

5 Now send men to Joppa, and send for Simon whose surname is Peter.

tunics . . . garments (v. 39)—close fitting undergarments and long outer robes

Simon, a tanner (v. 43)—Peter breaks down a cultural barrier by staying with a man whose job was to tan the hides of dead animals; such an occupation was considered unclean to the Jews and no doubt this Simon was shunned by the members of the local synagogue.

Italian regiment (10:1)—or "Italian cohort" (a legion was comprised of ten cohorts of six hundred men each)

feared God (v. 2)—a technical term to describe a Gentile who had abandoned his or her pagan religion and was, without becoming a full-fledged Jewish proselyte, attempting to worship the true God Yahweh

memorial (v. 4)—a remembrance; Cornelius's prayers, devotion, faith, and goodness were like a fragrant offering rising up to God

housetop to pray (v. 9)—The flat roofs of Jewish homes lent themselves to all kinds of worship.

all kinds of four-footed animals (v. 12)—both clean and unclean animals, according to Jewish dietary and ceremonial laws

kill and eat (v. 13)—The new covenant effectively ended the Old Testament dietary restrictions; God declared all animals clean, thus making possible a church comprised of both Jews and Gentiles.

6 *He is lodging with Simon, a tanner, whose house is by the sea. He will tell you what you must do."*

7 *And when the angel who spoke to him had departed, Cornelius called two of his household servants and a devout soldier from among those who waited on him continually.*

8 *So when he had explained all these things to them, he sent them to Joppa.*

9 *The next day, as they went on their journey and drew near the city, Peter went up on the housetop to pray, about the sixth hour.*

10 *Then he became very hungry and wanted to eat; but while they made ready, he fell into a trance*

11 *and saw heaven opened and an object like a great sheet bound at the four corners, descending to him and let down to the earth.*

12 *In it were all kinds of four-footed animals of the earth, wild beasts, creeping things, and birds of the air.*

13 *And a voice came to him, "Rise, Peter; kill and eat."*

14 *But Peter said, "Not so, Lord! For I have never eaten anything common or unclean."*

15 *And a voice spoke to him again the second time, "What God has cleansed you must not call common."*

16 *This was done three times. And the object was taken up into heaven again.*

17 *Now while Peter wondered within himself what this vision which he had seen meant, behold, the men who had been sent from Cornelius had made inquiry for Simon's house, and stood before the gate.*

18 *And they called and asked whether Simon, whose surname was Peter, was lodging there.*

19 *While Peter thought about the vision, the Spirit said to him, "Behold, three men are seeking you.*

20 *Arise therefore, go down and go with them, doubting nothing; for I have sent them."*

21 *Then Peter went down to the men who had been sent to him from Cornelius, and said, "Yes, I am he whom you seek. For what reason have you come?"*

22 *And they said, "Cornelius the centurion, a just man, one who fears God and has a good reputation among all the nation of the Jews, was divinely instructed by a holy angel to summon you to his house, and to hear words from you."*

23 *Then he invited them in and lodged them. On the next day Peter went away with them, and some brethren from Joppa accompanied him.*

invited them in (v. 23)—Self-respecting Jews did not invite Gentiles into their homes, much less soldiers of the hated Roman army.

24 *And the following day they entered Caesarea. Now Cornelius was waiting for them, and had called together his relatives and close friends.*

25 *As Peter was coming in, Cornelius met him and fell down at his feet and worshiped him.*

26 *But Peter lifted him up, saying, "Stand up; I myself am also a man."*

I myself am also a man (v. 26)—a reminder that only God deserves worship

27 *And as he talked with him, he went in and found many who had come together.*

28 *Then he said to them, "You know how unlawful it is for a Jewish man to keep company with or go to one of another nation. But God has shown me that I should not call any man common or unclean.*

unlawful (v. 28)—literally, "breaking a taboo"; his comments reveal his acceptance of Gentiles, a turnabout for one who had followed Jewish customs all his life

29 *Therefore I came without objection as soon as I was sent for. I ask, then, for what reason have you sent for me?"*

30 *So Cornelius said, "Four days ago I was fasting until this hour; and at the ninth hour I prayed in my house, and behold, a man stood before me in bright clothing,*

31 *and said, 'Cornelius, your prayer has been heard, and your alms are remembered in the sight of God.*

32 *Send therefore to Joppa and call Simon here, whose surname is Peter. He is lodging in the house of Simon, a tanner, by the sea. When he comes, he will speak to you.'*

33 *So I sent to you immediately, and you have done well to come. Now therefore, we are all present before God, to hear all the things commanded you by God."*

34 *Then Peter opened his mouth and said: "In truth I perceive that God shows no partiality.*

35 But in every nation whoever fears Him and works righteousness is accepted by Him.

36 The word which God sent to the children of Israel, preaching peace through Jesus Christ— He is Lord of all—

37 that word you know, which was proclaimed throughout all Judea, and began from Galilee after the baptism which John preached:

38 how God anointed Jesus of Nazareth with the Holy Spirit and with power, who went about doing good and healing all who were oppressed by the devil, for God was with Him.

39 And we are witnesses of all things which He did both in the land of the Jews and in Jerusalem, whom they killed by hanging on a tree.

40 Him God raised up on the third day, and showed Him openly,

41 not to all the people, but to witnesses chosen before by God, even to us who ate and drank with Him after He arose from the dead.

42 And He commanded us to preach to the people, and to testify that it is He who was ordained by God to be Judge of the living and the dead.

43 To Him all the prophets witness that, through His name, whoever believes in Him will receive remission of sins."

44 While Peter was still speaking these words, the Holy Spirit fell upon all those who heard the word.

45 And those of the circumcision who believed were astonished, as many as came with Peter, because the gift of the Holy Spirit had been poured out on the Gentiles also.

46 For they heard them speak with tongues and magnify God. Then Peter answered,

47 "Can anyone forbid water, that these should not be baptized who have received the Holy Spirit just as we have?"

48 And he commanded them to be baptized in the name of the Lord. Then they asked him to stay a few days.

11:1 *Now the apostles and brethren who were in Judea heard that the Gentiles had also received the word of God.*

2 *And when Peter came up to Jerusalem, those of the circumcision contended with him,*

3 *saying, "You went in to uncircumcised men and ate with them!"*

4 *But Peter explained it to them in order from the beginning, saying:*

5 *"I was in the city of Joppa praying; and in a trance I saw a vision, an object descending like a great sheet, let down from heaven by four corners; and it came to me.*

6 *When I observed it intently and considered, I saw four-footed animals of the earth, wild beasts, creeping things, and birds of the air.*

7 *And I heard a voice saying to me, 'Rise, Peter; kill and eat.'*

8 *But I said, 'Not so, Lord! For nothing common or unclean has at any time entered my mouth.'*

9 *But the voice answered me again from heaven, 'What God has cleansed you must not call common.'*

10 *Now this was done three times, and all were drawn up again into heaven.*

11 *At that very moment, three men stood before the house where I was, having been sent to me from Caesarea.*

12 *Then the Spirit told me to go with them, doubting nothing. Moreover these six brethren accompanied me, and we entered the man's house.*

13 *And he told us how he had seen an angel standing in his house, who said to him, 'Send men to Joppa, and call for Simon whose surname is Peter,*

14 *who will tell you words by which you and all your household will be saved.'*

15 *And as I began to speak, the Holy Spirit fell upon them, as upon us at the beginning.*

16 *Then I remembered the word of the Lord, how He said, 'John indeed baptized with water, but you shall be baptized with the Holy Spirit.'*

ate with them! (11:3)—The Jewish believers were outraged that Peter had committed such a breach of Jewish tradition.

your household (v. 14)—not a sweeping inclusion of infants, but a reference to all who could comprehend the gospel and believe

at the beginning (v. 15)—God confirmed the reality of Gentile salvation with the same phenomenon that occurred at Pentecost.

God has also granted the Gentiles repentance to life. (v. 18)—one of the most shocking admissions in Jewish history, but an event prophesied in the Old Testament

hand of the Lord (v. 21)—a reference to God's obvious power, either in judgment or in blessing; here it refers to blessing

Christians (v. 26)—initially a term of derision, meaning "of the party of Christ"

prophets (v. 27)—preachers of the New Testament

a great famine (v. 28)—Secular historians confirm this event as having happened in AD 45–46

17 If therefore God gave them the same gift as He gave us when we believed on the Lord Jesus Christ, who was I that I could withstand God?"

18 When they heard these things they became silent; and they glorified God, saying, "Then God has also granted to the Gentiles repentance to life."

19 Now those who were scattered after the persecution that arose over Stephen traveled as far as Phoenicia, Cyprus, and Antioch, preaching the word to no one but the Jews only.

20 But some of them were men from Cyprus and Cyrene, who, when they had come to Antioch, spoke to the Hellenists, preaching the Lord Jesus.

21 And the hand of the Lord was with them, and a great number believed and turned to the Lord.

22 Then news of these things came to the ears of the church in Jerusalem, and they sent out Barnabas to go as far as Antioch.

23 When he came and had seen the grace of God, he was glad, and encouraged them all that with purpose of heart they should continue with the Lord.

24 For he was a good man, full of the Holy Spirit and of faith. And a great many people were added to the Lord.

25 Then Barnabas departed for Tarsus to seek Saul.

26 And when he had found him, he brought him to Antioch. So it was that for a whole year they assembled with the church and taught a great many people. And the disciples were first called Christians in Antioch.

27 And in these days prophets came from Jerusalem to Antioch.

28 Then one of them, named Agabus, stood up and showed by the Spirit that there was going to be a great famine throughout all the world, which also happened in the days of Claudius Caesar.

29 Then the disciples, each according to his ability, determined to send relief to the brethren dwelling in Judea.

30 This they also did, and sent it to the elders by the hands of Barnabas and Saul.

12:1 Now about that time Herod the king stretched out his hand to harass some from the church.

2 Then he killed James the brother of John with the sword.

3 And because he saw that it pleased the Jews, he proceeded further to seize Peter also. Now it was during the Days of Unleavened Bread.

4 So when he had arrested him, he put him in prison, and delivered him to four squads of soldiers to keep him, intending to bring him before the people after Passover.

5 Peter was therefore kept in prison, but constant prayer was offered to God for him by the church.

6 And when Herod was about to bring him out, that night Peter was sleeping, bound with two chains between two soldiers; and the guards before the door were keeping the prison.

7 Now behold, an angel of the Lord stood by him, and a light shone in the prison; and he struck Peter on the side and raised him up, saying, "Arise quickly!" And his chains fell off his hands.

8 Then the angel said to him, "Gird yourself and tie on your sandals"; and so he did. And he said to him, "Put on your garment and follow me."

9 So he went out and followed him, and did not know that what was done by the angel was real, but thought he was seeing a vision.

10 When they were past the first and the second guard posts, they came to the iron gate that leads to the city, which opened to them of its own accord; and they went out and went down one street, and immediately the angel departed from him.

11 And when Peter had come to himself, he said, "Now I know for certain that the Lord has sent His angel, and has delivered me from the hand of Herod and from all the expectation of the Jewish people."

---

elders (v. 30)—pastors-overseers of the churches; these eventually occupied the leading role in the churches when the foundational apostles and prophets passed from the scene

Herod the king (12:1)—Herod Agrippa, son of Herod the Great, ruled from AD 37–44; his persecution of believers was an attempt to curry favor with the Jews.

James (v. 2)—the first of the apostles to be martyred

four squads (v. 4)—Each squad had four soldiers; at all times two guards were chained to Peter while the other two stood watch outside the cell.

12 So, when he had considered this, he came to the house of Mary, the mother of John whose surname was Mark, where many were gathered together praying.

13 And as Peter knocked at the door of the gate, a girl named Rhoda came to answer.

14 When she recognized Peter's voice, because of her gladness she did not open the gate, but ran in and announced that Peter stood before the gate.

15 But they said to her, "You are beside yourself!" Yet she kept insisting that it was so. So they said, "It is his angel."

16 Now Peter continued knocking; and when they opened the door and saw him, they were astonished.

17 But motioning to them with his hand to keep silent, he declared to them how the Lord had brought him out of the prison. And he said, "Go, tell these things to James and to the brethren." And he departed and went to another place.

18 Then, as soon as it was day, there was no small stir among the soldiers about what had become of Peter.

19 But when Herod had searched for him and not found him, he examined the guards and commanded that they should be put to death. And he went down from Judea to Caesarea, and stayed there.

20 Now Herod had been very angry with the people of Tyre and Sidon; but they came to him with one accord, and having made Blastus the king's personal aide their friend, they asked for peace, because their country was supplied with food by the king's country.

21 So on a set day Herod, arrayed in royal apparel, sat on his throne and gave an oration to them.

22 And the people kept shouting, "The voice of a god and not of a man!"

23 Then immediately an angel of the Lord struck him, because he did not give glory to God. And he was eaten by worms and died.

24 *But the word of God grew and multiplied.*
25 *And Barnabas and Saul returned from Jerusalem when they had fulfilled their ministry, and they also took with them John whose surname was Mark.*

1) Identify some of the highlights of Peter's ministry cited by Luke. Why were these events singled out and recorded?

_____

_____

_____

_____

2) What insights into Peter's character are found in chapters 9–12?

_____

_____

_____

_____

3) How did God sovereignly prepare Cornelius for what was to follow?

_____

_____

_____

_____

4) What did God do to prepare Peter for the momentous event of Gentile inclusion into the church?

_____

_____

_____

_____

GOING DEEPER

Paul later gave a theological explanation of the historical events recorded in Acts 10–11. Read Ephesians 2:11–22 for this explanation.

Exploring the Meaning

5) What is the gist of Paul's argument? What is he saying?

_____

_____

_____

_____

6) What truth was Peter beginning to grasp when he remarked that God shows no partiality (10:34)?

_____

_____

_____

_____

(Verses to consider: Deut. 10:17; 2 Chron. 19:7; Job 34:19; Rom. 2:11; 3:29–30; James 2:1)

7) What evidence or lines of argument did Peter use to calm his Jewish brothers who were alarmed and outraged by the influx of Gentiles into the church (11:1–18)?

_____

_____

_____

_____

Truth for Today

We are quick to exclude from our group those we deem undesirable—those who fail to flatter us, support our opinions, reinforce our prejudices, boost our pride, feed our egos, or whose style of life is significantly different. The world in general expresses its intolerance and bigotry in conflicts at every level, from silent prejudice to outright war. Even the church is not immune to this tendency. Those of another culture, skin color, social status, educational group, or income level often find themselves unwelcome in the church. Such intolerant exclusivism grieves the heart of the Lord Jesus Christ, whose purpose and prayer was that believers "may be one, as You, Father, are in Me, and I in You; that they also may be one in Us, that the world may believe that You sent Me" (John 17:21 NKJV).

Reflecting on the Text

8) Why do you think Luke included the events of chapter 12 in his record of the church? What lessons can be found in Herod's persecution of church leaders and his subsequent death?

_____

_____

_____

_____

9) How is God leading you to cross racial or cultural barriers with the love of Christ? What are some specific actions you can take?

_____

_____

_____

_____

10) In these chapters we see the extraordinary events that happen when the children of God call out in faith to their heavenly Father. On a scale of 1–10 (with 1 being "on life support" and 10 representing "I'm in communion with God all day every day") how would you rate the health of your prayer life?

_____

_____

_____

_____

11) What do you specifically need to change?

_____

_____

_____

_____

Personal Response

Write out additional reflections, questions you may have, or a prayer.

_____

_____

_____

_____

_____

_____

_____

_____

_____

_____

_____

_____

_____

_____

_____

_____

_____

_____

_____

_____

_____

_____

_____

_____

_____

7

PAUL'S FIRST MISSIONARY JOURNEY

DRAWING NEAR

As the early church grew, the first missionary movement was born. What images come to mind when you hear the word "missionary" or "missions"? Why?

_____

_____

_____

_____

THE CONTEXT

Beginning in Acts 13, Luke's history of the church focuses almost exclusively on outreach to the Gentiles and the consequent growth of the church "to the ends of the earth" (1:8). Here we find the Spirit's selection of Paul and Barnabas to become special missionaries, and we see a shift as Paul replaces Peter as the central figure in the book.

Paul's entourage (Barnabas and John Mark, at the very least) sets sail, stopping on Cyprus, where the messengers of Jesus confront a false prophet named Bar-Jesus. Then the mission moves north to Perga. For an unknown reason, John Mark abruptly leaves the venture and returns to Jerusalem. Paul and Barnabas continue inland to Antioch of Pisidia.

The initial reaction to Paul's preaching is favorable. But among the audience are a number of jealous Jewish leaders. Despite efforts by these men to discredit both Paul and his message, the assembled Gentiles eagerly embrace the gospel. This further incites the Jewish leaders, who are eventually able to stir up a mob that runs Paul and Barnabas out of town.

These events serve as a kind of microcosm of Paul's entire ministry: stiff opposition from most Jews and joyous acceptance of the gospel message by many Gentiles. Paul's joyful perseverance in the face of extreme persecution is testimony to the power of the Holy Spirit in a believer's life. These chapters not only demonstrate God's grace and faithfulness, but also set the stage for a coming controversy over the presence of newly converted Gentiles in a previously all-Jewish church.

KEYS TO THE TEXT

Barnabas: Barnabas, also Joses of Cyprus (Acts 4:36), was a member of the priestly tribe of the Levites and a native of the island of Cyprus. The apostles chose the perfect Christian name for Joses when they called him *Barnabas*—Son of Encouragement. Every appearance of Barnabas in Scripture finds him encouraging others in the faith. In fact, he serves as the supreme model for how to mentor young believers. Numerous churches can trace their beginnings back to the efforts of Barnabas, the Encourager. He became a close associate of Paul's and a prominent member of the church. (*What Does the Bible Say About—?*)

Evangelism: The word *evangelize* means the "to proclaim good tidings." More than any other individual, Paul was responsible for proclaiming the good news and spreading Christianity throughout the Roman Empire. Paul's method of Jewish evangelism throughout Acts was to prove from the Old Testament that Jesus was the Messiah. The "evangelist" was a gift of God to the early church (Eph. 4:11). These persons were not attached to any specific local church. They traveled over a wide geographical area, preaching to those to whom the Holy Spirit led them. The early disciples were also called evangelists (Acts 8:4) because they proclaimed the gospel. God does not call every believer to be an evangelist, but He calls every believer to be a witness. All Christians today may continue the witness of the early evangelists. As they spoke and wrote of Jesus, so may Christians bring His message to others today.

UNLEASHING THE TEXT

Read 13:1–14:28, noting the key words and definitions next to the passage.

prophets (v. 1)—preachers of God's word who instructed local congregations and occasionally received new revelation from God (though this function ended with the cessation of the temporary sign gifts)

Simeon . . . called Niger (v. 1)—"Niger" means "black." Simeon may have been African; there is no direct evidence to show this was the Simon who carried the cross of Christ.

ministered (v. 2)—the Greek word that in Scripture describes

Acts 13:1–14:28 (NKJV)

1 Now in the church that was at Antioch there were certain prophets and teachers: Barnabas, Simeon who was called Niger, Lucius of Cyrene, Manaen who had been brought up with Herod the tetrarch, and Saul.

2 As they ministered to the Lord and fasted, the Holy Spirit said, "Now separate to Me Barnabas and Saul for the work to which I have called them."

3 Then, having fasted and prayed, and laid hands on them, they sent them away.

4 So, being sent out by the Holy Spirit, they went down to Seleucia, and from there they sailed to Cyprus.

5 *And when they arrived in Salamis, they preached the word of God in the synagogues of the Jews. They also had John as their assistant.*

6 *Now when they had gone through the island to Paphos, they found a certain sorcerer, a false prophet, a Jew whose name was Bar-Jesus,*

7 *who was with the proconsul, Sergius Paulus, an intelligent man. This man called for Barnabas and Saul and sought to hear the word of God.*

8 *But Elymas the sorcerer (for so his name is translated) withstood them, seeking to turn the proconsul away from the faith.*

9 *Then Saul, who also is called Paul, filled with the Holy Spirit, looked intently at him*

10 *and said, "O full of all deceit and all fraud, you son of the devil, you enemy of all righteousness, will you not cease perverting the straight ways of the Lord?*

11 *And now, indeed, the hand of the Lord is upon you, and you shall be blind, not seeing the sun for a time." And immediately a dark mist fell on him, and he went around seeking someone to lead him by the hand.*

12 *Then the proconsul believed, when he saw what had been done, being astonished at the teaching of the Lord.*

13 *Now when Paul and his party set sail from Paphos, they came to Perga in Pamphylia; and John, departing from them, returned to Jerusalem.*

14 *But when they departed from Perga, they came to Antioch in Pisidia, and went into the synagogue on the Sabbath day and sat down.*

15 *And after the reading of the Law and the Prophets, the rulers of the synagogue sent to them, saying, "Men and brethren, if you have any word of exhortation for the people, say on."*

16 *Then Paul stood up, and motioning with his hand said, "Men of Israel, and you who fear God, listen:*

17 *The God of this people Israel chose our fathers, and exalted the people when they dwelt as strangers in the land of Egypt, and with an uplifted arm He brought them out of it.*

priestly service, implying that ministry is a form of worship

fasted (v. 2)—associated with fervent prayer and either the loss of appetite or the intentional decision to concentrate solely on spiritual issues

Cyprus (v. 4)—probably chosen because it was Barnabas' home and also the home to a large Jewish population

Paphos (v. 6)—the capital of Cyprus

sorcerer (v. 6)—a magician who dabbled in the occult; the name Elymas is a transliteration of the Arabic word for magician

Perga in Pamphylia (v. 13)—in Asia Minor (modern-day Turkey)

John, departing from them (v. 13)—Whatever Mark's reasons, they were not accepted by Paul (15:38). This incident led to a rift between Paul and Barnabas (15:36–40) that was obviously resolved much later (see 2 Tim. 4:11).

Antioch in Pisidia (v. 14)—not to be confused with Syrian Antioch, location of the first Gentile church

a man after My own heart (v. 22)—David was obviously a sinner; this description implies his hunger for God and his humble willingness to acknowledge sin, repent, and seek forgiveness.

according to the promise (v. 23)—Old Testament prophecy points to the Messiah as a descendant of David.

rulers (v. 27)—the supposed experts in the Old Testament, including the scribes, Pharisees, Sadducees, and priests

tree . . . tomb (v. 29)—The Old Testament predicted Christ's crucifixion (Ps. 22; Num. 34) and his burial (Isa. 53:9).

God raised (v. 30)—the ultimate proof that Jesus is the Messiah

witnesses (v. 31)—more than five hundred (see 1 Cor. 15:5–8)

18 *Now for a time of about forty years He put up with their ways in the wilderness.*

19 *And when He had destroyed seven nations in the land of Canaan, He distributed their land to them by allotment.*

20 *"After that He gave them judges for about four hundred and fifty years, until Samuel the prophet.*

21 *And afterward they asked for a king; so God gave them Saul the son of Kish, a man of the tribe of Benjamin, for forty years.*

22 *And when He had removed him, He raised up for them David as king, to whom also He gave testimony and said, 'I have found David the son of Jesse, a man after My own heart, who will do all My will.'*

23 *From this man's seed, according to the promise, God raised up for Israel a Savior—Jesus—*

24 *after John had first preached, before His coming, the baptism of repentance to all the people of Israel.*

25 *And as John was finishing his course, he said, 'Who do you think I am? I am not He. But behold, there comes One after me, the sandals of whose feet I am not worthy to loose.'*

26 *"Men and brethren, sons of the family of Abraham, and those among you who fear God, to you the word of this salvation has been sent.*

27 *For those who dwell in Jerusalem, and their rulers, because they did not know Him, nor even the voices of the Prophets which are read every Sabbath, have fulfilled them in condemning Him.*

28 *And though they found no cause for death in Him, they asked Pilate that He should be put to death.*

29 *Now when they had fulfilled all that was written concerning Him, they took Him down from the tree and laid Him in a tomb.*

30 *But God raised Him from the dead.*

31 *He was seen for many days by those who came up with Him from Galilee to Jerusalem, who are His witnesses to the people.*

32 *And we declare to you glad tidings— that promise which was made to the fathers.*

33 *God has fulfilled this for us their children, in that He has raised up Jesus. As it is also written in the second Psalm: 'You are My Son, Today I have begotten You.'*

34 *And that He raised Him from the dead, no more to return to corruption, He has spoken thus: 'I will give you the sure mercies of David.'*

35 *Therefore He also says in another Psalm: 'You will not allow Your Holy One to see corruption.'*

36 *"For David, after he had served his own generation by the will of God, fell asleep, was buried with his fathers, and saw corruption;*

37 *but He whom God raised up saw no corruption.*

38 *Therefore let it be known to you, brethren, that through this Man is preached to you the forgiveness of sins;*

39 *and by Him everyone who believes is justified from all things from which you could not be justified by the law of Moses.*

40 *Beware therefore, lest what has been spoken in the prophets come upon you:*

41 *'Behold, you despisers, Marvel and perish! For I work a work in your days, A work which you will by no means believe, Though one were to declare it to you.' "*

42 *So when the Jews went out of the synagogue, the Gentiles begged that these words might be preached to them the next Sabbath.*

43 *Now when the congregation had broken up, many of the Jews and devout proselytes followed Paul and Barnabas, who, speaking to them, persuaded them to continue in the grace of God.*

44 *On the next Sabbath almost the whole city came together to hear the word of God.*

45 *But when the Jews saw the multitudes, they were filled with envy; and contradicting and blaspheming, they opposed the things spoken by Paul.*

46 *Then Paul and Barnabas grew bold and said, "It was necessary that the word of God should be spoken to you first; but since you reject it, and judge yourselves unworthy of everlasting life, behold, we turn to the Gentiles.*

you could not be justified by the law of Moses. (v. 39)—Attempting to keep the law of Moses never freed anyone from his or her sins.

devout proselytes (v. 43)—full converts to Judaism who had been circumcised

continue in the grace of God (v. 43)—those who are truly saved persevere in the grace of God.

to you first (v. 46)—God offered the plan of salvation to the Jews first (see Luke 24:47 and Rom. 1:16).

we turn to the Gentiles (v. 46)—because of the Jewish rejection of the gospel, however, the Gentiles have always been part of God's plan.

appointed to eternal life (v. 48)—one of Scripture's clearest statements on the sovereignty of God; He chooses us—not the other way around

shook off the dust (v. 51)—a symbolic act demonstrating condemnation; devout Jews would attempt to avoid even bringing Gentile dust into Israel; Paul and Barnabas were equating these "devout" Jews with pagan Gentiles

granting signs and wonders (14:3)—Such demonstrations of divine power confirmed the message of Paul and Barnabas.

apostles (v. 4)—Barnabas was not truly an apostle; the word can be translated "messenger" and that is likely the meaning here.

47 For so the Lord has commanded us: 'I have set you as a light to the Gentiles, That you should be for salvation to the ends of the earth.'"

48 Now when the Gentiles heard this, they were glad and glorified the word of the Lord. And as many as had been appointed to eternal life believed.

49 And the word of the Lord was being spread throughout all the region.

50 But the Jews stirred up the devout and prominent women and the chief men of the city, raised up persecution against Paul and Barnabas, and expelled them from their region.

51 But they shook off the dust from their feet against them, and came to Iconium.

52 And the disciples were filled with joy and with the Holy Spirit.

14:1 Now it happened in Iconium that they went together to the synagogue of the Jews, and so spoke that a great multitude both of the Jews and of the Greeks believed.

2 But the unbelieving Jews stirred up the Gentiles and poisoned their minds against the brethren.

3 Therefore they stayed there a long time, speaking boldly in the Lord, who was bearing witness to the word of His grace, granting signs and wonders to be done by their hands.

4 But the multitude of the city was divided: part sided with the Jews, and part with the apostles.

5 And when a violent attempt was made by both the Gentiles and Jews, with their rulers, to abuse and stone them,

6 they became aware of it and fled to Lystra and Derbe, cities of Lycaonia, and to the surrounding region.

7 And they were preaching the gospel there.

8 And in Lystra a certain man without strength in his feet was sitting, a cripple from his mother's womb, who had never walked.

9 This man heard Paul speaking. Paul, observing him intently and seeing that he had faith to be healed,

10 said with a loud voice, "Stand up straight on your feet!" And he leaped and walked.

11 Now when the people saw what Paul had done, they raised their voices, saying in the Lycaonian language, "The gods have come down to us in the likeness of men!"

12 And Barnabas they called Zeus, and Paul, Hermes, because he was the chief speaker.

13 Then the priest of Zeus, whose temple was in front of their city, brought oxen and garlands to the gates, intending to sacrifice with the multitudes.

14 But when the apostles Barnabas and Paul heard this, they tore their clothes and ran in among the multitude, crying out

15 and saying, "Men, why are you doing these things? We also are men with the same nature as you, and preach to you that you should turn from these useless things to the living God, who made the heaven, the earth, the sea, and all things that are in them,

16 who in bygone generations allowed all nations to walk in their own ways.

17 Nevertheless He did not leave Himself without witness, in that He did good, gave us rain from heaven and fruitful seasons, filling our hearts with food and gladness."

18 And with these sayings they could scarcely restrain the multitudes from sacrificing to them.

19 Then Jews from Antioch and Iconium came there; and having persuaded the multitudes, they stoned Paul and dragged him out of the city, supposing him to be dead.

20 However, when the disciples gathered around him, he rose up and went into the city. And the next day he departed with Barnabas to Derbe.

21 And when they had preached the gospel to that city and made many disciples, they returned to Lystra, Iconium, and Antioch,

22 strengthening the souls of the disciples, exhorting them to continue in the faith, and saying, "We must through many tribulations enter the kingdom of God."

23 So when they had appointed elders in every church, and prayed with fasting, they commended them to the Lord in whom they had believed.

"The gods have come . . . " (v. 11)—A pagan folklore tradition said that the gods Zeus and Hermes had once visited Lystra incognito; the locals thought this might be another instance of "divine" visitation.

tore their clothes (v. 14)—a Jewish expression of horror and revulsion at blasphemy

did not leave Himself without witness (v. 17)—Paul cited God's providence and His creative power, not Scripture, in addressing this Gentile audience.

they stoned Paul . . . supposing him to be dead (v. 19)—Paul did not die and resurrect; the mob erroneously assumed Paul to be dead.

73

24 *And after they had passed through Pisidia, they came to Pamphylia.*

25 *Now when they had preached the word in Perga, they went down to Attalia.*

From there (v. 26)—Thus ended Paul's first missionary journey.

26 *From there they sailed to Antioch, where they had been commended to the grace of God for the work which they had completed.*

27 *Now when they had come and gathered the church together, they reported all that God had done with them, and that He had opened the door of faith to the Gentiles.*

28 *So they stayed there a long time with the disciples.*

1) If possible, look at a map of Palestine during Paul's time. Find Antioch and trace Paul's journey.

_____

_____

2) This passage indicates that the original missionary enterprise was preceded by a time of fasting and prayer. What happened as a result?

_____

_____

3) What is the purpose of fasting? What are the benefits?

_____

_____

(Verses to consider: Neh. 1:4; Ps. 35:13; Dan. 9:3; Matt. 6:16–17; 17:21; Luke 2:27)

4) What happened when Paul and Barnabas encountered Bar-Jesus (13:6)?

_____

_____

5) At Pisidian Antioch, Paul preached a message that is recorded in 13:16–41. What did Paul say in his closing words about the issue of justification? How did this square with the typical Jewish understanding of salvation?

_____

_____

(Verses to consider: Rom. 3:28; 1 Cor. 1:30; Gal. 2:16; 3:11; Phil. 3:9; Col. 2:13–14)

6) Note all the wonders and miracles done during this time. Would you characterize Paul's first mission effort as successful or not? Why?

_____

_____

GOING DEEPER

Read Psalm 2, a messianic psalm that depicts the world's hatred for the Son of God (and by implication, those who would follow Him).

EXPLORING THE MEANING

7) What about the apostle's message so infuriated the Jews? What was the result of their fierce anger?

_____

_____

8) Paul and Barnabas never seemed surprised and they certainly never retreated when they encountered opposition. What was the secret to their boldness and perseverance?

_____

_____

9) Acts 13:48 makes clear that in salvation, God chooses the person; the person does not choose God. The matter of human will and divine election is so inscrutable, so incomprehensible to our minds, as to demand that we believe both without being able to comprehend how they fit together in God's mind. What questions about the doctrine of election trouble you most? How do you resolve them?

_____

_____

10) Why did Paul and Barnabas make the effort to revisit the cities in which they had previously ministered? What implications are here for modern-day Christians and churches?

_____

_____

Truth for Today

Conflict will often occur when the true gospel is preached today. The gospel does not gather everyone together, nor is it a generally tolerable opinion that nonbelievers can take or leave. Instead it splits people, dividing the penitent from the hardhearted, the saved from the unsaved, the righteous from the reprobate, those who love its truth from those who reject it.

Reflecting on the Text

11) In what ways do you see people today getting angry because of the gospel? What lies behind these reactions?

_____

_____

12) What character qualities do you most appreciate in Paul and Barnabas? To what degree are those same traits evident in your life? In what areas do you need to grow?

_____

_____

13) The ministry pictured in Acts 13 and 14 is all-encompassing. Paul and Barnabas did not simply preach sermons—they poured out their lives so that others might know Christ and grow in Him. Think about how involved you are in some sort of ministry. What is stopping you from coming alongside other people and helping them grow spiritually? What specific steps can you take this week to be bolder for Christ?

_____

_____

_____

Personal Response

Write out additional reflections, questions you may have, or a prayer.

_____

_____

_____

_____

8

THE JERUSALEM COUNCIL

Acts 15:1-35

DRAWING NEAR

Think about the religious upbringing you had. Was it legalistic and rigid? What did you appreciate about it? What were its weaknesses?

_____

_____

_____

How do you define "legalism"? What are some examples of legalism among Christians today?

_____

_____

_____

THE CONTEXT

The flood of Gentile believers into the church surfaced underlying attitudes of pride and prejudice. Some legalistic Jews even tried to demand that the new converts be circumcised. Fierce arguing among the parties resulted in the first church council. At Jerusalem the apostles and elders convened to consider the relationship between Jewish believers and Gentile Christians, between the Mosaic Law and the gospel of grace.

Looking at the Old Testament book of Amos (as expounded by James, leader of the proceedings) and in light of the sovereign experiences of both Peter and Paul, the council concluded that Gentiles were equal partners with the Jews in God's eternal plan. Further, the council ruled that salvation depended solely on belief in Jesus, not on keeping the law of Moses.

The Jerusalem Council summarized its decision regarding Gentile circumcision in a letter. Judas and Silas carried this letter to Antioch. Paul and Barnabas accompanied these specially chosen messengers. The letter instructed the Gentile converts to strictly avoid idolatry, immorality, and eating the meat of unbled animals—activities common among the Gentiles that were especially offensive to Jewish sensibilities. This directive brought joy to the believers at Antioch. The

Jerusalem entourage stayed with the Gentile church for a while, strengthening the believers and teaching God's Word.

KEYS TO THE TEXT

Legalism: The strict, self-dependent trust in one's own efforts to perform to the level of divine morality—human attempts to become acceptable to God by means of human efforts. The Jews' own Scriptures did not teach salvation by obedience to God's law, much less by obedience to the many man-made laws and traditions that had been devised. Nevertheless, members of the Jewish majority in Jesus' and Paul's day placed their trust in those man-made regulations. In fact, most of them had more faith in rabbinical traditions than in God's divinely revealed law in Scripture. Before his conversion, Paul was himself the epitome of Jewish legalism. The spirit of legalism was carried into the church by many Jews who had taken on the name of Christ. They were referred to as Judaizers, because they attempted to add to the gospel the legalistic requirements of the Old Testament, such as circumcision and obedience to the Sabbath laws.

The Christian's obligations to God are not another form of legalism. The person who is genuinely saved has a new and divine nature that is, by definition, attuned to God's will. When he lives by his new nature in the power of the Spirit, his desire is God's desire and no compulsion is involved.

UNLEASHING THE TEXT

Read 15:1–35, noting the key words and definitions next to the passage.

Acts 15:1–35 (NKJV)

certain men (v. 1)—Judaizers, that is, false teachers who were self-appointed guardians of legalism, teaching a doctrine of salvation by works

Unless you are circumcised . . . you cannot be saved. (v. 1)—This was, briefly summarized, the heresy propagated by the Judaizers.

up to Jerusalem (v. 2)—The city of Jerusalem has a higher elevation than the surrounding area; thus travelers literally go "up" to enter the city.

elders (v. 2)—the leaders of the Jerusalem church

1 *And certain men came down from Judea and taught the brethren, "Unless you are circumcised according to the custom of Moses, you cannot be saved."*

2 *Therefore, when Paul and Barnabas had no small dissension and dispute with them, they determined that Paul and Barnabas and certain others of them should go up to Jerusalem, to the apostles and elders, about this question.*

3 *So, being sent on their way by the church, they passed through Phoenicia and Samaria, describing the conversion of the Gentiles; and they caused great joy to all the brethren.*

4 *And when they had come to Jerusalem, they were*

received by the church and the apostles and the elders; and they reported all things that God had done with them.

5 But some of the sect of the Pharisees who believed rose up, saying, "It is necessary to circumcise them, and to command them to keep the law of Moses."

6 Now the apostles and elders came together to consider this matter.

7 And when there had been much dispute, Peter rose up and said to them: "Men and brethren, you know that a good while ago God chose among us, that by my mouth the Gentiles should hear the word of the gospel and believe.

8 So God, who knows the heart, acknowledged them by giving them the Holy Spirit, just as He did to us,

9 and made no distinction between us and them, purifying their hearts by faith.

10 Now therefore, why do you test God by putting a yoke on the neck of the disciples which neither our fathers nor we were able to bear?

11 But we believe that through the grace of the Lord Jesus Christ we shall be saved in the same manner as they."

12 Then all the multitude kept silent and listened to Barnabas and Paul declaring how many miracles and wonders God had worked through them among the Gentiles.

13 And after they had become silent, James answered, saying, "Men and brethren, listen to me:

14 Simon has declared how God at the first visited the Gentiles to take out of them a people for His name.

15 And with this the words of the prophets agree, just as it is written:

16 'After this I will return And will rebuild the tabernacle of David, which has fallen down; I will rebuild its ruins, And I will set it up;

17 So that the rest of mankind may seek the LORD, Even all the Gentiles who are called by My name, Says the LORD who does all these things.'

all things (v. 4)—The report by Paul and Barnabas was thorough and should have been enough evidence of God's sovereign selection of the Gentiles.

Peter rose up (v. 7)—Peter's speech, the first of three at the council, is a strong defense of salvation by faith. In essence, he reminded everyone that God had not required circumcision of previous Gentile converts (see 10–11). If that were so, how could the legalists demand this act for salvation?

giving them the Holy Spirit (v. 8)—proof of the genuineness of their salvation

a yoke (v. 10)—the idea is that the legalists were placing a heavy burden or load on these new converts

Barnabas and Paul (v. 12)—The missionaries spoke next and reported on God's obvious work among the Gentiles during their just-completed trip.

James answered (v. 13)—the third address of the conference; also a ringing defense of salvation by faith

the words of the prophets agree (v. 15)—The quote is from Amos—the scene is of the millennium—and the text makes no mention of Gentiles becoming Jewish proselytes; the idea is if Gentiles can be saved without becoming Jews in the age to come, they do not need to become Jews in the present age.

79

18 "Known to God from eternity are all His works.

19 Therefore I judge that we should not trouble those
from among the Gentiles who are turning to God,

20 but that we write to them to abstain from things
polluted by idols, from sexual immorality, from
things strangled, and from blood.

21 For Moses has had throughout many generations
those who preach him in every city, being read in
the synagogues every Sabbath."

22 Then it pleased the apostles and elders, with the
whole church, to send chosen men of their own
company to Antioch with Paul and Barnabas,
namely, Judas who was also named Barsabas, and
Silas, leading men among the brethren.

23 They wrote this letter by them: The apostles, the
elders, and the brethren, To the brethren who
are of the Gentiles in Antioch, Syria, and Cilicia:
Greetings.

24 Since we have heard that some who went out
from us have troubled you with words, unsettling
your souls, saying, "You must be circumcised
and keep the law"—to whom we gave no such
commandment—

25 it seemed good to us, being assembled with one
accord, to send chosen men to you with our beloved
Barnabas and Paul,

26 men who have risked their lives for the name of our
Lord Jesus Christ.

27 We have therefore sent Judas and Silas, who will
also report the same things by word of mouth.

28 For it seemed good to the Holy Spirit, and to us,
to lay upon you no greater burden than these
necessary things:

29 that you abstain from things offered to idols, from
blood, from things strangled, and from sexual
immorality. If you keep yourselves from these, you
will do well. Farewell.

30 So when they were sent off, they came to Antioch;
and when they had gathered the multitude together,
they delivered the letter.

31 *When they had read it, they rejoiced over its encouragement.*

32 *Now Judas and Silas, themselves being prophets also, exhorted and strengthened the brethren with many words.*

33 *And after they had stayed there for a time, they were sent back with greetings from the brethren to the apostles.*

34 *However, it seemed good to Silas to remain there.*

35 *Paul and Barnabas also remained in Antioch, teaching and preaching the word of the Lord, with many others also.*

1) What conflict threatened to tear apart the early church?

_____

_____

_____

2) What did first-century believers do to attempt to resolve this bitter debate?

_____

_____

_____

3) How did the events of the Jerusalem Council unfold? What is your impression of these men?

_____

_____

_____

4) What decisions were eventually reached? Upon what evidence did the leaders make their decision?

_____

_____

_____

Going Deeper

For insight into another tough situation in the church at Corinth, read 1 Corinthians 8:1–13.

Exploring the Meaning

5) How (if at all) does this situation in Corinth compare to the situation in Jerusalem? What counsel did Paul give the church?

_____

_____

_____

_____

6) Read Romans 14:14–21. How do you think legalism differs from voluntary self-restriction due to the law of love?

_____

_____

_____

_____

7) How were the council's decisions received by the Jews? By the Gentiles?

_____

_____

_____

_____

Truth for Today

Throughout its history the church's leaders have met to settle doctrinal issues. Historians point to seven ecumenical councils in the church's early history, especially the Councils of Nicea (AD 325) and Chalcedon (AD 451). Yet the most important council was the first one—the Jerusalem Council—because it established the answer to the most vital doctrinal question of all: "What must a person do to be saved?" The apostles and elders defied efforts to impose legalism and ritualism as necessary prerequisites for salvation. They forever affirmed that salvation is totally by grace through faith in Christ alone.

Reflecting on the Text

8) R. C. H. Lenski has written: "To add anything to Christ as being necessary to salvation, say circumcision or any human work of any kind, is to deny that Christ is the complete Savior, is to put something human on a par with him. That is fatal. A bridge to heaven that is built of 99/100 of Christ and even only 1/100 of anything human breaks down at the joint and ceases to be a bridge." What are some of the common misconceptions about salvation today? In what human elements do many people trust to save them?

_____

_____

_____

_____

9) What principles for conflict resolution among believers do you see in chapter 15? Which ones can you use this week?

_____

_____

_____

_____

10) How would history have been affected and how might your life be different if the leaders of the first-century church had not addressed the issue of salvation as it did in chapter 15?

_____

_____

_____

11) How can a believer discern between guidelines and rules that are truly biblical and those that are merely cultural or human-made?

_____

_____

_____

_____

PERSONAL RESPONSE

Write out additional reflections, questions you may have, or a prayer.

DRAWING NEAR

In this study of the book of Acts, what have you learned about God thus far?

_____

_____

_____

What have you learned about yourself?

_____

_____

_____

THE CONTEXT

Luke records that when the time came for a second missionary journey, Barnabas and Paul had a sharp disagreement concerning John Mark. Barnabas wanted to take his nephew, but Paul refused, citing the young man's desertion during the first evangelistic endeavor. Thus, in the sovereignty of God, two missionary teams were formed: Paul and Silas, and Barnabas and Mark. The two teams departed Antioch in two directions. No further word is given regarding the results of Barnabas' and Mark's evangelistic efforts. Paul and Silas returned to the churches of Asia Minor.

At Lystra Paul met Timothy, who became a beloved and dependable colleague. Forbidden by the Holy Spirit to go into the provinces of Asia and Bithynia, Paul and his companions were directed, instead, through Mysia to the city of Troas. There Paul had a divine vision instructing him to go to Macedonia. In response to this Macedonian call, Paul and his assistants immediately set sail. At Philippi (in what is now northern Greece) they encountered a group of God-fearing women. They journeyed on to Thessalonica, where the response to the gospel message was typical: a revival among the Greeks and a riot at the hands of the Jewish leaders. But God continued to use persecution and opposition to spread the good news of forgiveness and eternal life through Jesus Christ. The ruckus in Thessalonica pushed Paul and Silas to Berea where they found a very teachable and receptive Greek audience. In a short time, hostile Jews came from Thessalonica to attack Paul's work in Berea. This succeeded only in getting the great evangelist to Athens.

At Mars Hill, Paul demonstrated his ability to be all things to all people, preaching the gospel of the resurrected Christ by using concepts and terms the Athenian philosophers could easily grasp. Some scoffed at his message, but others indicated their interest in hearing more. Moving on to Corinth, Paul met Priscilla and Aquila, a married couple (and fellow tentmakers) who proved to be faithful partners in the gospel (see Rom. 16:3; 1 Cor. 16:19; 2 Tim. 4:19). Eventually Paul went to Syria, made a brief stop in Ephesus, and then continued on to the church at Jerusalem to report on his activity. This marked the end of Paul's second missionary journey.

KEYS TO THE TEXT

Visions and God's Will: Paul's Macedonian vision was the second of six visions received by Paul. Visions are experiences similar to dreams through which supernatural insight or awareness is given by revelation. The difference between a dream and a vision is that dreams occur only during sleep, while visions can happen while a person is awake (Dan. 10:7). In the Bible, people who had visions were filled with a special consciousness of God. The most noteworthy examples in the Old Testament of recipients of visions are Ezekiel and Daniel. Visions in the New Testament are most prominent in the Gospel of Luke, the book of Acts, and the book of Revelation. The purpose of visions was to give guidance and direction to God's servants and to foretell the future. (*Nelson's New Illustrated Bible Dictionary*)

Athens: The cultural center of Greece. At its zenith, Athens was home to the most renowned philosophers in history, including Socrates, Plato, and Aristotle, who was arguably the most influential philosopher of all. Two other significant philosophers taught there: Epicurus, founder of Epicureanism, and Zeno, founder of Stoicism—two of the dominant philosophies in that day. Epicurean philosophy taught that the chief end of man was the avoidance of pain. Epicureans were materialists—they did not deny the existence of God, but they believed He was not involved with the affairs of men. When a person died, they believed one's body and soul disintegrated. Stoic philosophy taught self-mastery—that the goal in life was to reach a place of indifference to pleasure or pain. Athens was also the religious center of Greece—virtually every deity known to man could be worshiped there. Paul viewed Athens as a city of lost humanity, all doomed to a Christ-less eternity because of rampant pagan idolatry.

UNLEASHING THE TEXT

Read 15:36–18:22, noting the key words and definitions next to the passage.

Acts 15:36–18:22 (NKJV)

36 Then after some days Paul said to Barnabas, "Let us now go back and visit our brethren in every city where we have preached the word of the Lord, and see how they are doing."

37 Now Barnabas was determined to take with them John called Mark.

38 But Paul insisted that they should not take with them the one who had departed from them in Pamphylia, and had not gone with them to the work.

39 Then the contention became so sharp that they parted from one another. And so Barnabas took Mark and sailed to Cyprus;

40 but Paul chose Silas and departed, being commended by the brethren to the grace of God.

41 And he went through Syria and Cilicia, strengthening the churches.

16:1 Then he came to Derbe and Lystra. And behold, a certain disciple was there, named Timothy, the son of a certain Jewish woman who believed, but his father was Greek.

2 He was well spoken of by the brethren who were at Lystra and Iconium.

3 Paul wanted to have him go on with him. And he took him and circumcised him because of the Jews who were in that region, for they all knew that his father was Greek.

4 And as they went through the cities, they delivered to them the decrees to keep, which were determined by the apostles and elders at Jerusalem.

5 So the churches were strengthened in the faith, and increased in number daily.

6 Now when they had gone through Phrygia and the region of Galatia, they were forbidden by the Holy Spirit to preach the word in Asia.

see how they are doing (v. 36)— Paul recognized that he had a responsibility to help new believers grow in the faith.

contention . . . parted (v. 39)— This sharp disagreement resulted in two ministry teams. The men eventually reconciled.

Silas (v. 40)—An ideal companion for Paul, Silas had prophetic gifts, Jewish credentials, and Roman citizenship.

Syria and Cilicia (v. 41)—Paul may have founded churches in these cities before his association with the Antioch church (see Gal. 1:21).

a certain disciple . . . Timothy (16:1)—Paul's "true child in the faith" (1 Tim. 1:2) who eventually became Paul's right-hand man; he too had a Jew-Gentile heritage (an asset for a missionary)

circumcised him (v. 3)—in order to make him more acceptable to the Jews and give him access to the synagogues

decrees (v. 4)—the ruling of the Jerusalem Council

Holy Spirit . . . Asia (v. 6)— Paul was divinely prohibited from carrying out his plan to minister in Asia Minor.

87

vision (v. 9)—the second of six visions that Luke records Paul as having received

vision (v. 9)—the second of six visions that Luke records Paul as having received

Macedonia (v. 9)—across the Aegean Sea from Troas, on the Greek mainland (that is, in Europe)

we (v. 10)—Luke had obviously joined Paul, Silas, and Timothy by this point in the journey.

Philippi (v. 12)—Located ten miles from the port city of Neapolis, this Roman colony was named for Philip II of Macedon, the father of Alexander the Great.

to the riverside (v. 13)—Evidently the Jewish community did not have the minimum of ten men required to form a synagogue, so the group met near the Gangites River.

seller of purple (v. 14)—Purple dye was expensive, so purple fabrics were bought by the wealthy at a premium price. Lydia was a prosperous businesswoman.

The Lord opened her heart (v. 14)—proof of the sovereignty of God in salvation

a spirit of divination (v. 16)—literally, "a python spirit," an expression from Greek mythology where a python guarded the oracle at Delphi; this girl was a medium involved in demonic activities

the Most High God (v. 17)—literally, El Elyon, an Old Testament title for God referring to His absolute sovereignty

7 *After they had come to Mysia, they tried to go into Bithynia, but the Spirit did not permit them.*

8 *So passing by Mysia, they came down to Troas.*

9 *And a vision appeared to Paul in the night. A man of Macedonia stood and pleaded with him, saying, "Come over to Macedonia and help us."*

10 *Now after he had seen the vision, immediately we sought to go to Macedonia, concluding that the Lord had called us to preach the gospel to them.*

11 *Therefore, sailing from Troas, we ran a straight course to Samothrace, and the next day came to Neapolis,*

12 *and from there to Philippi, which is the foremost city of that part of Macedonia, a colony. And we were staying in that city for some days.*

13 *And on the Sabbath day we went out of the city to the riverside, where prayer was customarily made; and we sat down and spoke to the women who met there.*

14 *Now a certain woman named Lydia heard us. She was a seller of purple from the city of Thyatira, who worshiped God. The Lord opened her heart to heed the things spoken by Paul.*

15 *And when she and her household were baptized, she begged us, saying, "If you have judged me to be faithful to the Lord, come to my house and stay." So she persuaded us.*

16 *Now it happened, as we went to prayer, that a certain slave girl possessed with a spirit of divination met us, who brought her masters much profit by fortune-telling.*

17 *This girl followed Paul and us, and cried out, saying, "These men are the servants of the Most High God, who proclaim to us the way of salvation."*

18 *And this she did for many days. But Paul, greatly annoyed, turned and said to the spirit, "I command you in the name of Jesus Christ to come out of her." And he came out that very hour.*

19 *But when her masters saw that their hope of profit*

was gone, they seized Paul and Silas and dragged them into the marketplace to the authorities.

20 And they brought them to the magistrates, and said, "These men, being Jews, exceedingly trouble our city;

21 and they teach customs which are not lawful for us, being Romans, to receive or observe."

22 Then the multitude rose up together against them; and the magistrates tore off their clothes and commanded them to be beaten with rods.

23 And when they had laid many stripes on them, they threw them into prison, commanding the jailer to keep them securely.

24 Having received such a charge, he put them into the inner prison and fastened their feet in the stocks.

25 But at midnight Paul and Silas were praying and singing hymns to God, and the prisoners were listening to them.

26 Suddenly there was a great earthquake, so that the foundations of the prison were shaken; and immediately all the doors were opened and everyone's chains were loosed.

27 And the keeper of the prison, awaking from sleep and seeing the prison doors open, supposing the prisoners had fled, drew his sword and was about to kill himself.

28 But Paul called with a loud voice, saying, "Do yourself no harm, for we are all here."

29 Then he called for a light, ran in, and fell down trembling before Paul and Silas.

30 And he brought them out and said, "Sirs, what must I do to be saved?"

31 So they said, "Believe on the Lord Jesus Christ, and you will be saved, you and your household."

32 Then they spoke the word of the Lord to him and to all who were in his house.

33 And he took them the same hour of the night and washed their stripes. And immediately he and all his family were baptized.

Jews . . . trouble our city (v. 20)— Such anti-Semitism may have been a factor in the Emperor Claudius's edict that expelled all the Jews from Rome (see 18:2).

magistrates . . . commanded them to be beaten (v. 22)— These judges illegally punished Paul, as they had not been given a hearing, nor had they been convicted of a crime.

inner prison . . . in the stocks (v. 24)—in the most secure part of the prison with their legs spread apart and locked in a painful position

about to kill himself (v. 27)— Roman soldiers who allowed a prisoner to escape were executed; this man obviously preferred suicide over such a fate.

you and your household (v. 31)—that is, all who were old enough to comprehend the gospel and believe it

34 Now when he had brought them into his house, he set food before them; and he rejoiced, having believed in God with all his household.

35 And when it was day, the magistrates sent the officers, saying, "Let those men go."

36 So the keeper of the prison reported these words to Paul, saying, "The magistrates have sent to let you go. Now therefore depart, and go in peace."

37 But Paul said to them, "They have beaten us openly, uncondemned Romans, and have thrown us into prison. And now do they put us out secretly? No indeed! Let them come themselves and get us out."

38 And the officers told these words to the magistrates, and they were afraid when they heard that they were Romans.

39 Then they came and pleaded with them and brought them out, and asked them to depart from the city.

40 So they went out of the prison and entered the house of Lydia; and when they had seen the brethren, they encouraged them and departed.

17:1 Now when they had passed through Amphipolis and Apollonia, they came to Thessalonica, where there was a synagogue of the Jews.

2 Then Paul, as his custom was, went in to them, and for three Sabbaths reasoned with them from the Scriptures,

3 explaining and demonstrating that the Christ had to suffer and rise again from the dead, and saying, "This Jesus whom I preach to you is the Christ."

4 And some of them were persuaded; and a great multitude of the devout Greeks, and not a few of the leading women, joined Paul and Silas.

5 But the Jews who were not persuaded, becoming envious, took some of the evil men from the marketplace, and gathering a mob, set all the city in an uproar and attacked the house of Jason, and sought to bring them out to the people.

6 But when they did not find them, they dragged Jason and some brethren to the rulers of the city,

crying out, "These who have turned the world upside down have come here too.

7 Jason has harbored them, and these are all acting contrary to the decrees of Caesar, saying there is another king—Jesus."

8 And they troubled the crowd and the rulers of the city when they heard these things.

9 So when they had taken security from Jason and the rest, they let them go.

10 Then the brethren immediately sent Paul and Silas away by night to Berea. When they arrived, they went into the synagogue of the Jews.

11 These were more fair-minded than those in Thessalonica, in that they received the word with all readiness, and searched the Scriptures daily to find out whether these things were so.

12 Therefore many of them believed, and also not a few of the Greeks, prominent women as well as men.

13 But when the Jews from Thessalonica learned that the word of God was preached by Paul at Berea, they came there also and stirred up the crowds.

14 Then immediately the brethren sent Paul away, to go to the sea; but both Silas and Timothy remained there.

15 So those who conducted Paul brought him to Athens; and receiving a command for Silas and Timothy to come to him with all speed, they departed.

16 Now while Paul waited for them at Athens, his spirit was provoked within him when he saw that the city was given over to idols.

17 Therefore he reasoned in the synagogue with the Jews and with the Gentile worshipers, and in the marketplace daily with those who happened to be there.

18 Then certain Epicurean and Stoic philosophers encountered him. And some said, "What does this babbler want to say?" Others said, "He seems to be a proclaimer of foreign gods," because he preached to them Jesus and the resurrection.

contrary to the decrees of Caesar (v. 7)—To acknowledge allegiance to any king but Caesar was a serious crime in the Roman Empire.

security (v. 9)—They posted bond, forfeitable in the event of further trouble.

Athens (v. 15)—the cultural, religious, and philosophical center of Greece

idols (v. 16)—Athens was a hotbed of paganism.

Epicurean and Stoic philosophers (v. 18)—The Epicureans sought to avoid pain and seek pleasure; the Stoics advocated self-denial.

babbler (v. 18)—Literally, "seed-picker;" the label means they viewed Paul as a shallow person who borrowed bits and pieces from many different philosophical systems.

THE UNKNOWN GOD (v. 23)—The Athenians at least acknowledged the existence of some kind of supernatural power or force; Paul used this fact as a springboard in his attempt to introduce them to the one true God.

God, who made the world (v. 24)—This teaching contradicted both Epicureanism (which stated that matter is eternal) and Stoicism (which stated that God was one with the universe and could not, therefore, have created Himself.

seek the Lord (v. 27)—in response to God's self-revelation as creator, ruler, and controller of the world

in Him we . . . have our being (v. 28)—a quote from the Cretan poet Epimenides

offspring of God (v. 29)—a quote from Aratus, who hailed from Paul's home region of Cilicia

19 And they took him and brought him to the Areopagus, saying, "May we know what this new doctrine is of which you speak?

20 For you are bringing some strange things to our ears. Therefore we want to know what these things mean."

21 For all the Athenians and the foreigners who were there spent their time in nothing else but either to tell or to hear some new thing.

22 Then Paul stood in the midst of the Areopagus and said, "Men of Athens, I perceive that in all things you are very religious;

23 for as I was passing through and considering the objects of your worship, I even found an altar with this inscription: TO THE UNKNOWN GOD. Therefore, the One whom you worship without knowing, Him I proclaim to you:

24 God, who made the world and everything in it, since He is Lord of heaven and earth, does not dwell in temples made with hands.

25 Nor is He worshiped with men's hands, as though He needed anything, since He gives to all life, breath, and all things.

26 And He has made from one blood every nation of men to dwell on all the face of the earth, and has determined their preappointed times and the boundaries of their dwellings,

27 so that they should seek the Lord, in the hope that they might grope for Him and find Him, though He is not far from each one of us;

28 for in Him we live and move and have our being, as also some of your own poets have said, 'For we are also His offspring.'

29 Therefore, since we are the offspring of God, we ought not to think that the Divine Nature is like gold or silver or stone, something shaped by art and man's devising.

30 Truly, these times of ignorance God overlooked, but now commands all men everywhere to repent,

31 because He has appointed a day on which He will judge the world in righteousness by the Man whom He has ordained. He has given assurance of this to all by raising Him from the dead."

32 And when they heard of the resurrection of the dead, some mocked, while others said, "We will hear you again on this matter."

33 So Paul departed from among them.

34 However, some men joined him and believed, among them Dionysius the Areopagite, a woman named Damaris, and others with them.

18:1 After these things Paul departed from Athens and went to Corinth.

2 And he found a certain Jew named Aquila, born in Pontus, who had recently come from Italy with his wife Priscilla (because Claudius had commanded all the Jews to depart from Rome); and he came to them.

3 So, because he was of the same trade, he stayed with them and worked; for by occupation they were tentmakers.

4 And he reasoned in the synagogue every Sabbath, and persuaded both Jews and Greeks.

5 When Silas and Timothy had come from Macedonia, Paul was compelled by the Spirit, and testified to the Jews that Jesus is the Christ.

6 But when they opposed him and blasphemed, he shook his garments and said to them, "Your blood be upon your own heads; I am clean. From now on I will go to the Gentiles."

7 And he departed from there and entered the house of a certain man named Justus, one who worshiped God, whose house was next door to the synagogue.

8 Then Crispus, the ruler of the synagogue, believed on the Lord with all his household. And many of the Corinthians, hearing, believed and were baptized.

9 Now the Lord spoke to Paul in the night by a vision, "Do not be afraid, but speak, and do not keep silent;

10 for I am with you, and no one will attack you to hurt you; for I have many people in this city."

resurrection of the dead (v. 32)—a doctrine flatly rejected by Greek philosophy

Corinth (18:1)—The leading commercial and political center in Greece on a major trade route, Corinth was a city seething with immorality.

Priscilla and Aquila (v. 2)—a husband-and-wife team who became two of Paul's most valued colleagues in ministry; probably already believers when they met Paul

commanded (v. 2)—This decree was issued in AD 49.

Your blood be upon your own heads (v. 6)—Paul held his enemies completely responsible for blaspheming Christ and rejecting the gospel.

Justus (v. 7)—a Roman, possibly Gaius Titius Justus (see Rom. 16:23) who was interested in the gospel

vision (v. 9)—Paul's third in a series of six recorded by Luke

I have many people in this city. (v. 10)—God had appointed a number of people in Corinth for salvation; these elect would come to faith through Paul's preaching.

a year and six months (v. 11)—Paul's longest stay anywhere, except Ephesus

contrary to the law (v. 13)—a charge that Christianity, viewed then by the Romans as simply a sect within the tolerated religion of Judaism, was actually an aberration and should not be tolerated; a serious charge that could have resulted in a ban on Christianity throughout the Roman Empire; Gallio refused to get caught up in what he viewed as an internal squabble within Judaism

Sosthenes (v. 17)—The Greeks may have been venting general hostility or they may have been angry at his unsuccessful prosecution of Paul; Sosthenes later became a believer (see 1 Cor. 1:1).

taken a vow (v. 18)—an expression of gratitude (see Num. 6:2–5, 13–21) lasting a predetermined amount of time

down to Antioch (v. 22)—the official end of Paul's second missionary journey

11 *And he continued there a year and six months, teaching the word of God among them.*

12 *When Gallio was proconsul of Achaia, the Jews with one accord rose up against Paul and brought him to the judgment seat,*

13 *saying, "This fellow persuades men to worship God contrary to the law."*

14 *And when Paul was about to open his mouth, Gallio said to the Jews, "If it were a matter of wrongdoing or wicked crimes, O Jews, there would be reason why I should bear with you.*

15 *But if it is a question of words and names and your own law, look to it yourselves; for I do not want to be a judge of such matters."*

16 *And he drove them from the judgment seat.*

17 *Then all the Greeks took Sosthenes, the ruler of the synagogue, and beat him before the judgment seat. But Gallio took no notice of these things.*

18 *So Paul still remained a good while. Then he took leave of the brethren and sailed for Syria, and Priscilla and Aquila were with him. He had his hair cut off at Cenchrea, for he had taken a vow.*

19 *And he came to Ephesus, and left them there; but he himself entered the synagogue and reasoned with the Jews.*

20 *When they asked him to stay a longer time with them, he did not consent,*

21 *but took leave of them, saying, "I must by all means keep this coming feast in Jerusalem; but I will return again to you, God willing." And he sailed from Ephesus.*

22 *And when he had landed at Caesarea, and gone up and greeted the church, he went down to Antioch.*

1) What motivated Paul to go on a second missionary journey? Where did he go and what did he do?

_____

_____

_____

_____

(Verses to consider: Matt. 28:18–20; Eph. 4:12–13; Phil. 1:8; Col. 1:28)

2) How did Paul and his team end up in Philippi, and what key events happened there?

_____

_____

_____

_____

3) What strategies did Paul use to speak to the philosophers at Athens? How is this address different from the message he preached to the devout Jewish audience as recorded in 13:16–41?

_____

_____

_____

_____

Going Deeper

The Old Testament often illuminates the New Testament. Read Isaiah 44:9–20 for an Old Testament perspective on idolatry.

Exploring the Meaning

4) What does the Isaiah passage say about idolatry? Why is it so foolish?

_____

_____

_____

5) Why do you think idols were so popular everywhere Paul went? In what ways do people worship "idols" today?

_____

_____

_____

6) Paul spoke to the Athenians about God as Creator. Why is this such an important truth to believe?

_____

_____

_____

7) It seems as though everywhere Paul went either a riot or a revival broke out. Acts 17:6 confirms this, recording that the apostolic band was described as men "who have turned the world upside down." Why do you think Paul was such a lightning rod? What was his secret for ministerial success?

_____

_____

_____

Truth for Today

Courage must be coupled with the proper content if a believer is to shake the world. To have the right message, but not the boldness to proclaim it, renders it useless. On the other hand, to boldly proclaim error, as the cults do, causes even greater harm. Proclaiming the truth with great boldness, as Paul did, cannot help but change the world.

Reflecting on the Text

8) Today in most places religious tolerance is valued and all religions are to be respected. To say anyone is wrong or right is to be "narrow-minded." How do you think Paul would respond to this statement?

_____

_____

9) Review 16:22–25. How can a Christian choose joy in the midst of unpleasant circumstances?

_____

_____

_____

10) Do you know someone who is trapped by Satan (like the fortune-teller of 16:16–18) or who is blinded to the truth (like the philosophers of 17:16–32)? As you ponder their spiritual state, what thoughts and feelings do you have? What is God calling you to do?

_____

_____

_____

11) What is one quality from the life of Paul that you would like to emulate? Ask God to begin to work this into your heart and life.

_____

_____

_____

PERSONAL RESPONSE

Write out additional reflections, questions you may have, or a prayer.

_____

_____

_____

_____

_____

_____

_____

_____

_____

ADDITIONAL NOTES

10

PAUL'S THIRD MISSIONARY JOURNEY

DRAWING NEAR

Paul was given unique gifts and a unique purpose to tirelessly preach the good news. What is your unique purpose and gift(s) to use for the kingdom of God?

_____

_____

Take time to reflect on this, and ask God to clarify your purpose and passion.

_____

_____

THE CONTEXT

Evidence from Paul's epistles suggests the great apostle launched out on his third missionary trip in an attempt to undo the damage caused among the churches by numerous opponents of the gospel. Beginning at Antioch, Paul journeyed through Galatia and Phrygia, eventually coming to Ephesus on the west coast of Asia Minor.

Paul's ministry in Ephesus lasted more than two years and was marked by an obvious movement of God's Spirit. Luke records that "the word of the Lord grew mightily and prevailed." Following a riot instigated by area tradesmen, who saw the spread of Christianity as a threat to their livelihood selling silver idols of the goddess Diana, Paul ventured through Macedonia and into Achaia. In Athens, Paul was again divinely protected from a murderous plot at the hands of the Jews. Arriving at Miletus, Paul summoned the elders of the Ephesian church to bid them farewell. This emotional discourse reveals Paul's pastoral heart, and it records the presence of a well-trained group of disciples who would be able to carry the message of Christ throughout Asia.

As Paul visited Tyre and Caesarea, prophecies were given, warning him of certain imprisonment if he journeyed to Jerusalem. Unmoved, Paul determined to complete his mission even if it meant dying "for the name of the Lord Jesus." God's sovereignty is the underlying theme in this section. This truth becomes even more apparent when later chapters reveal how this Jerusalem visit ultimately paved the way for Paul's "all expenses paid" trip to Rome!

Keys to the Text

Ephesus: It is likely that the gospel was first brought to Ephesus by Priscilla and Aquila, an exceptionally gifted couple, who were left there by Paul on his second missionary journey. Located at the mouth of the Cayster River, on the east side of the Aegean Sea, the city of Ephesus was perhaps best known for its magnificent temple of Artemis, or Diana, one of the seven wonders of the ancient world. It was also an important political, educational, and commercial center, ranking with Alexandria in Egypt, and Antioch of Pisidia, in southern Asia Minor.

God's Sovereignty: A theological term that refers to the unlimited power of God, who has sovereign control over the affairs of nature and history. The Bible declares that God is working out His sovereign plan of redemption for the world and that the conclusion is certain. The story of redemption from Genesis to Revelation is possible only because the sovereign God loves the created world, fallen though it is, and is able to do something about it. Without the sovereign love of the Father ministered to us through the Son and the Holy Spirit, there would be no real human freedom and no hope of everlasting life.

The apostles' persecution and trials did not discourage them. They took confidence in God's sovereign control of all events, even their sufferings. God's sovereignty is not the sovereignty of a tyrant, but the loving providence of a gracious God. The believer who doesn't live in the confidence of God's sovereignty will lack God's peace and be left to the chaos of a troubled heart. But our confident trust in the Lord will allow us to thank Him in the midst of trials because we have God's peace on duty to protect our hearts. (*Nelson's New Illustrated Bible Dictionary*)

Unleashing the Text

Read 18:23–21:16, noting the key words and definitions next to the passage.

Acts 18:23–21:16 (NKJV)

Apollos (v. 24)—an Old Testament saint and follower of John the Baptist; following the further instruction of Priscilla and Aquila, he became a powerful Christian preacher

the way of the Lord (v. 25)—an Old Testament phrase describing the broad spiritual and moral commands of God, not necessarily the explicit Christian faith

baptism of John (v. 25)—John's baptism prepared people for the

23 *After he had spent some time there, he departed and went over the region of Galatia and Phrygia in order, strengthening all the disciples.*

24 *Now a certain Jew named Apollos, born at Alexandria, an eloquent man and mighty in the Scriptures, came to Ephesus.*

25 *This man had been instructed in the way of the Lord; and being fervent in spirit, he spoke and taught accurately the things of the Lord, though he knew only the baptism of John.*

26 So he began to speak boldly in the synagogue. When Aquila and Priscilla heard him, they took him aside and explained to him the way of God more accurately.

27 And when he desired to cross to Achaia, the brethren wrote, exhorting the disciples to receive him; and when he arrived, he greatly helped those who had believed through grace;

28 for he vigorously refuted the Jews publicly, showing from the Scriptures that Jesus is the Christ.

19:1 And it happened, while Apollos was at Corinth, that Paul, having passed through the upper regions, came to Ephesus. And finding some disciples

2 he said to them, "Did you receive the Holy Spirit when you believed?" So they said to him, "We have not so much as heard whether there is a Holy Spirit."

3 And he said to them, "Into what then were you baptized?" So they said, "Into John's baptism."

4 Then Paul said, "John indeed baptized with a baptism of repentance, saying to the people that they should believe on Him who would come after him, that is, on Christ Jesus."

5 When they heard this, they were baptized in the name of the Lord Jesus.

6 And when Paul had laid hands on them, the Holy Spirit came upon them, and they spoke with tongues and prophesied.

7 Now the men were about twelve in all.

8 And he went into the synagogue and spoke boldly for three months, reasoning and persuading concerning the things of the kingdom of God.

9 But when some were hardened and did not believe, but spoke evil of the Way before the multitude, he departed from them and withdrew the disciples, reasoning daily in the school of Tyrannus.

10 And this continued for two years, so that all who dwelt in Asia heard the word of the Lord Jesus, both Jews and Greeks.

11 Now God worked unusual miracles by the hands of Paul,

Messiah's arrival. Apollos accepted that message, but he did not grasp basic Christian truths like the significance of Christ's death and resurrection, the ministry of the Holy Spirit, etc.

the way of God more accurately (v. 26)—a fuller explanation of the Christian faith

the brethren wrote (v. 27)—Letters of commendation were common in the early church.

some disciples (19:1)—followers of John the Baptist, hence Old Testament seekers; the word "disciple" means learner or follower and does not always refer to one who possesses saving faith

"Did you receive the Holy Spirit . . . " (v. 2)—The question reflects Paul's uncertainty about their spiritual state; they knew about John's baptism, but had not received Christian baptism.

believe on . . . Christ Jesus (v. 4)—John instructed them about Jesus Christ, not how to receive the Spirit.

baptized (v. 5)—Although required of believers, baptism does not save.

spoke with tongues (v. 6)—During this transitional period in salvation history, such an experience (similar to the events of chapters 2 and 10) served as proof that the Spirit, of whom they had not heard, was now indwelling them.

hardened (v. 9)—The Greek word refers to defiance against God.

the school of Tyrannus (v. 9)—either the owner of the hall, or a philosopher who spoke there; the name means "our Tyrant" and may be a nickname given by weary pupils; Paul was allowed to use the facility when it was free in the afternoons

two years (v. 10)—Paul taught here for two of the three years he was in Ephesus (see 20:31).

unusual miracles (v. 11)—to confirm and validate Paul's apostolic authority

Jesus . . . Paul I know (v. 15)—The demon recognized that these charlatan exorcists had no authority over him (unlike Jesus and the apostle Paul).

books (v. 19)—of magic spells, worth an astonishing sum of money; by burning them, the new believers would not be able to resume their secret rites

I must also see Rome. (v. 21)—Paul understood the strategic importance of the imperial city; effective ministry there would result in worldwide impact.

silver shrines (v. 24)—household idols of the goddess Diana (also known as Artemis); the sale of these was quite lucrative

12 *so that even handkerchiefs or aprons were brought from his body to the sick, and the diseases left them and the evil spirits went out of them.*

13 *Then some of the itinerant Jewish exorcists took it upon themselves to call the name of the Lord Jesus over those who had evil spirits, saying, "We exorcise you by the Jesus whom Paul preaches."*

14 *Also there were seven sons of Sceva, a Jewish chief priest, who did so.*

15 *And the evil spirit answered and said, "Jesus I know, and Paul I know; but who are you?"*

16 *Then the man in whom the evil spirit was leaped on them, overpowered them, and prevailed against them, so that they fled out of that house naked and wounded.*

17 *This became known both to all Jews and Greeks dwelling in Ephesus; and fear fell on them all, and the name of the Lord Jesus was magnified.*

18 *And many who had believed came confessing and telling their deeds.*

19 *Also, many of those who had practiced magic brought their books together and burned them in the sight of all. And they counted up the value of them, and it totaled fifty thousand pieces of silver.*

20 *So the word of the Lord grew mightily and prevailed.*

21 *When these things were accomplished, Paul purposed in the Spirit, when he had passed through Macedonia and Achaia, to go to Jerusalem, saying, "After I have been there, I must also see Rome."*

22 *So he sent into Macedonia two of those who ministered to him, Timothy and Erastus, but he himself stayed in Asia for a time.*

23 *And about that time there arose a great commotion about the Way.*

24 *For a certain man named Demetrius, a silversmith, who made silver shrines of Diana, brought no small profit to the craftsmen.*

25 *He called them together with the workers of similar occupation, and said: "Men, you know that we have our prosperity by this trade.*

26 *Moreover you see and hear that not only at Ephesus, but throughout almost all Asia, this Paul has persuaded and turned away many people, saying that they are not gods which are made with hands.*

27 *So not only is this trade of ours in danger of falling into disrepute, but also the temple of the great goddess Diana may be despised and her magnificence destroyed, whom all Asia and the world worship."*

28 *Now when they heard this, they were full of wrath and cried out, saying, "Great is Diana of the Ephesians!"*

29 *So the whole city was filled with confusion, and rushed into the theater with one accord, having seized Gaius and Aristarchus, Macedonians, Paul's travel companions.*

30 *And when Paul wanted to go in to the people, the disciples would not allow him.*

31 *Then some of the officials of Asia, who were his friends, sent to him pleading that he would not venture into the theater.*

32 *Some therefore cried one thing and some another, for the assembly was confused, and most of them did not know why they had come together.*

assembly (v. 32)—The frenzied mob gathered in the theater, while the Asian leaders and Ephesian believers tried to discourage Paul from speaking and inciting the crowd further.

33 *And they drew Alexander out of the multitude, the Jews putting him forward. And Alexander motioned with his hand, and wanted to make his defense to the people.*

34 *But when they found out that he was a Jew, all with one voice cried out for about two hours, "Great is Diana of the Ephesians!"*

35 *And when the city clerk had quieted the crowd, he said: "Men of Ephesus, what man is there who does not know that the city of the Ephesians is temple guardian of the great goddess Diana, and of the image which fell down from Zeus?*

city clerk (v. 35)—in effect, the mayor

the image which fell . . . Zeus (v. 35)—a likely reference to a meteor, believed to be a divine sign

36 *Therefore, since these things cannot be denied, you ought to be quiet and do nothing rashly.*

37 *For you have brought these men here who are neither robbers of temples nor blasphemers of your goddess.*

38 *Therefore, if Demetrius and his fellow craftsmen have a case against anyone, the courts are open and*

there are proconsuls. Let them bring charges against one another.

39 But if you have any other inquiry to make, it shall be determined in the lawful assembly.

40 For we are in danger of being called in question for today's uproar, there being no reason which we may give to account for this disorderly gathering."

41 And when he had said these things, he dismissed the assembly.

20:1 After the uproar had ceased, Paul called the disciples to himself, embraced them, and departed to go to Macedonia.

2 Now when he had gone over that region and encouraged them with many words, he came to Greece

3 and stayed three months. And when the Jews plotted against him as he was about to sail to Syria, he decided to return through Macedonia.

4 And Sopater of Berea accompanied him to Asia—also Aristarchus and Secundus of the Thessalonians, and Gaius of Derbe, and Timothy, and Tychicus and Trophimus of Asia.

5 These men, going ahead, waited for us at Troas.

6 But we sailed away from Philippi after the Days of Unleavened Bread, and in five days joined them at Troas, where we stayed seven days.

7 Now on the first day of the week, when the disciples came together to break bread, Paul, ready to depart the next day, spoke to them and continued his message until midnight.

8 There were many lamps in the upper room where they were gathered together.

9 And in a window sat a certain young man named Eutychus, who was sinking into a deep sleep. He was overcome by sleep; and as Paul continued speaking, he fell down from the third story and was taken up dead.

10 But Paul went down, fell on him, and embracing him said, "Do not trouble yourselves, for his life is in him."

11 Now when he had come up, had broken bread and eaten, and talked a long while, even till daybreak, he departed.

Jews plotted against him (20:3)—probably a plan to kill Paul on his journey to Palestine, resulting in a change of travel plans

first day of the week (v. 7)—Sunday, the day the church gathered to worship and celebrate Christ's resurrection

young man (v. 9)—likely between 7 and 14; the fumes of the lamps (v. 8) may have induced his sleepy state

12 *And they brought the young man in alive, and they were not a little comforted.*

13 *Then we went ahead to the ship and sailed to Assos, there intending to take Paul on board; for so he had given orders, intending himself to go on foot.*

14 *And when he met us at Assos, we took him on board and came to Mitylene.*

15 *We sailed from there, and the next day came opposite Chios. The following day we arrived at Samos and stayed at Trogyllium. The next day we came to Miletus.*

16 *For Paul had decided to sail past Ephesus, so that he would not have to spend time in Asia; for he was hurrying to be at Jerusalem, if possible, on the Day of Pentecost.*

17 *From Miletus he sent to Ephesus and called for the elders of the church.*

18 *And when they had come to him, he said to them: "You know, from the first day that I came to Asia, in what manner I always lived among you,*

19 *serving the Lord with all humility, with many tears and trials which happened to me by the plotting of the Jews;*

20 *how I kept back nothing that was helpful, but proclaimed it to you, and taught you publicly and from house to house,*

21 *testifying to Jews, and also to Greeks, repentance toward God and faith toward our Lord Jesus Christ.*

22 *And see, now I go bound in the spirit to Jerusalem, not knowing the things that will happen to me there,*

23 *except that the Holy Spirit testifies in every city, saying that chains and tribulations await me.*

24 *But none of these things move me; nor do I count my life dear to myself, so that I may finish my race with joy, and the ministry which I received from the Lord Jesus, to testify to the gospel of the grace of God.*

25 *"And indeed, now I know that you all, among whom I have gone preaching the kingdom of God, will see my face no more.*

26 *Therefore I testify to you this day that I am innocent of the blood of all men.*

with many tears (v. 19)—Paul wept for the lost (Rom. 9:2–3), for the immature (1 Cor. 2:4), and for those endangered by false teachers (20:29–31).

from house to house (v. 20)—Paul's ministry included personal instruction in individual homes.

Holy Spirit testifies (v. 23)—Paul knew he faced danger ahead, but he was marked by a deep sense of duty.

whole counsel of God (v. 27)—the entire plan and purpose of God for salvation in all its fullness

overseers (v. 28)—same as elders and pastors; those who protect and lead

savage wolves (v. 29)—the true nature of the false teachers

build you up (v. 32)—The Bible is the source of spiritual growth.

these hands . . . provided for my necessities (v. 34)—Though Paul had every right to earn a living from the gospel, he often would support himself with his tentmaking skill.

fell on Paul's neck (v. 37)—a common biblical way of expressing extreme emotion

departed (21:1)—literally, "to tear away," describing the emotional anguish of Paul's departure

27 For I have not shunned to declare to you the whole counsel of God.

28 Therefore take heed to yourselves and to all the flock, among which the Holy Spirit has made you overseers, to shepherd the church of God which He purchased with His own blood.

29 For I know this, that after my departure savage wolves will come in among you, not sparing the flock.

30 Also from among yourselves men will rise up, speaking perverse things, to draw away the disciples after themselves.

31 Therefore watch, and remember that for three years I did not cease to warn everyone night and day with tears.

32 "So now, brethren, I commend you to God and to the word of His grace, which is able to build you up and give you an inheritance among all those who are sanctified.

33 I have coveted no one's silver or gold or apparel.

34 Yes, you yourselves know that these hands have provided for my necessities, and for those who were with me.

35 I have shown you in every way, by laboring like this, that you must support the weak. And remember the words of the Lord Jesus, that He said, 'It is more blessed to give than to receive.' "

36 And when he had said these things, he knelt down and prayed with them all.

37 Then they all wept freely, and fell on Paul's neck and kissed him,

38 sorrowing most of all for the words which he spoke, that they would see his face no more. And they accompanied him to the ship.

21:1 Now it came to pass, that when we had departed from them and set sail, running a straight course we came to Cos, the following day to Rhodes, and from there to Patara.

2 And finding a ship sailing over to Phoenicia, we went aboard and set sail.

3 When we had sighted Cyprus, we passed it on the left, sailed to Syria, and landed at Tyre; for there the ship was to unload her cargo.

4 *And finding disciples, we stayed there seven days. They told Paul through the Spirit not to go up to Jerusalem.*

5 *When we had come to the end of those days, we departed and went on our way; and they all accompanied us, with wives and children, till we were out of the city. And we knelt down on the shore and prayed.*

6 *When we had taken our leave of one another, we boarded the ship, and they returned home.*

7 *And when we had finished our voyage from Tyre, we came to Ptolemais, greeted the brethren, and stayed with them one day.*

8 *On the next day we who were Paul's companions departed and came to Caesarea, and entered the house of Philip the evangelist, who was one of the seven, and stayed with him.*

9 *Now this man had four virgin daughters who prophesied.*

10 *And as we stayed many days, a certain prophet named Agabus came down from Judea.*

11 *When he had come to us, he took Paul's belt, bound his own hands and feet, and said, "Thus says the Holy Spirit, 'So shall the Jews at Jerusalem bind the man who owns this belt, and deliver him into the hands of the Gentiles.' "*

12 *Now when we heard these things, both we and those from that place pleaded with him not to go up to Jerusalem.*

13 *Then Paul answered, "What do you mean by weeping and breaking my heart? For I am ready not only to be bound, but also to die at Jerusalem for the name of the Lord Jesus."*

14 *So when he would not be persuaded, we ceased, saying, "The will of the Lord be done."*

15 *And after those days we packed and went up to Jerusalem.*

16 *Also some of the disciples from Caesarea went with us and brought with them a certain Mnason of Cyprus, an early disciple, with whom we were to lodge.*

disciples (v. 4)—The church at Tyre had been founded by the Jerusalem believers who had fled from the persecution instigated by Paul (see 11:19).

virgin daughters . . . prophesied (v. 9)—That they were virgins may indicate a calling by God into special ministry (see 1 Cor. 7:34). The nature and extent of their prophetic gifts is not disclosed by Luke.

belt (v. 11)—Old Testament prophets often acted out their prophecies; here Agabus' action foreshadowed Paul's arrest and imprisonment.

for the name (v. 13)—The name of the Lord Jesus represents all that He is.

1) Describe Apollos and his strengths and gifts.

_____

_____

_____

2) What evidence suggests that the men encountered by Paul in 19:1–7 were not yet saved?

_____

_____

_____

(Verses to consider: Mark 2:18; Luke 5:33; 1 Cor. 6:19; 12:13; 2 Cor. 6:16; Eph. 1:13; Rom. 8:9; Jude 19)

3) How did Paul spend the bulk of his time in Ephesus? What were the results of his ministry there (19:9–41)?

_____

_____

_____

_____

GOING DEEPER

Read 1 Thessalonians 2:1–12 for more about Paul's relationship with his spiritual children in Christ.

EXPLORING THE MEANING

4) What does Paul say in 1 Thessalonians 2 about his ministry motives and practices?

_____

_____

_____

5) What are some of the concrete and practical ways that the apostle Paul demonstrated a pastor's heart for those to whom he ministered? (See Acts 19 and 20)

_____

_____

_____

6) Why do you suppose Luke included the story of Eutychus in his record (20:7–12)? What do you learn from that incident?

_____

_____

7) Review 20:22–23. How was Paul able to stay motivated in the face of such unrelenting opposition and certain persecution?

_____

_____

Truth for Today

The weapon that Christians are to wield in their personal battle with the forces of darkness is "the sword of the Spirit, which is the word of God" (Eph. 6:17 NKJV). As it is through the power of the Word alone that the intellectual fortresses of Satan fall, Christians by that truth can successfully battle Satan and his demon hosts. Even the book of Acts, which records the apostles' evangelistic ministry, emphasizes the preaching of the Word over signs, wonders, miracles, and exorcisms. And in Acts 6:4 the apostles defined the priorities of their ministry in the church: "We will devote ourselves to prayer, and to the ministry of the word."

Reflecting on the Text

8) How well do you know the Bible? Do you have a good grasp of the Scripture? Why or why not? What steps can you take this week to become a better student of God's Word?

_____

_____

9) Christianity did not face fierce opposition in Ephesus until it began affecting the sale of silver items. Suddenly things got very ugly! In many ways this attitude is still in place. Token religiosity is OK, as long as it does not result in an adverse financial effect. The minute it hurts the pocketbook, beliefs take a back seat to economic concerns. In what specific ways are you sometimes tempted to value material prosperity over spiritual purity?

_____

_____

10) The new believers in Ephesus wisely made a clean break with their past by burning occult objects from their old life before Christ (19:18–20). Is there anything from your past that you are hanging on to that may be hampering your walk with the Lord? What do you need to do to make a clean break?

_____

_____

_____

_____

_____

Personal Response

Write out additional reflections, questions you may have, or a prayer.

_____

_____

_____

_____

_____

_____

_____

_____

_____

_____

_____

_____

_____

_____

_____

_____

THE TRIALS OF THE MINISTRY

11

Acts 21:17–26:32

DRAWING NEAR

When was the last time you were able to share your testimony with someone else? What happened?

_____

_____

THE CONTEXT

In this lengthy section dominated by charges and trials and defense testimony, Luke recorded Paul's arrival at Jerusalem, where he was warmly welcomed by believers. Due to the strong Jewish animosity toward Paul, however, James and the elders encouraged the apostle to participate in a public Jewish ceremony of purification at the temple. Such an act, they felt, would quell the false rumors circulating that he was actively undermining the Mosaic Law.

This attempt to placate the enemies of the gospel was an utter failure, with a group of Jews from Asia making false and highly inflammatory accusations against the apostle. Only the quick action of a detachment of Roman soldiers saved Paul from being beaten to death by an angry mob.

Paul addressed the crowd, presenting his credentials as a devout Jew trained under the highly respected rabbi Gamaliel. He even described his unlikely encounter with the risen Christ on the Damascus Road. But when he mentioned Christ's command to go "far from here to the Gentiles" (22:21), the mob erupted in anger. Barely escaping a flogging, Paul was brought before the Jewish high council. The atmosphere was highly charged, and the high priest ordered Paul slapped after he had uttered the first sentence of his defense!

Acts 23–26 records three trials of Paul, the first before Felix the Roman governor in Caesarea. The second trial was two years later before the new governor, Festus. During this trial Paul used his rights as a Roman citizen and asked for a hearing before Caesar. Third, King Agrippa, in Caesarea with his sister Bernice for a political visit, then became embroiled in the controversy over Paul. Festus found Paul's testimony absurd; Agrippa found it pointed and a bit too personal. Nevertheless, Paul took advantage of this situation to share his encounter with Christ and his fervent belief in the truth of the gospel. He did not let the goal (reaching Rome) obscure opportunities that surfaced along the way to his destination.

111

KEYS TO THE TEXT

James and the Elders: James was the brother of Jesus and head of the Jerusalem church. James, along with the rest of Jesus' brothers, initially rejected Him (John 7:5). Later, however, he came to believe in Jesus as Israel's Messiah. Such was his godliness and zeal that he soon became the recognized head of the Jerusalem church. Though not an apostle, he was a prominent leader in the early church, and James held that position until his martyrdom about AD 62. The mention of elders indicates that the apostles, often away on evangelistic work, had turned over rule of the Jerusalem church to them. Some have speculated that there were seventy elders, paralleling the Sanhedrin. Given the large size of the Jerusalem church, there probably were at least that many. God had decreed that after the apostles were gone, the church was to be ruled by elders.

King Agrippa. This was Herod Agrippa II, son of the Herod who killed James and imprisoned Peter. He was the last of the Herods, who play a prominent role in New Testament history. His great-uncle, Herod Antipas, was the Herod of the Gospels, while his great-grandfather, Herod the Great, ruled at the time Jesus was born. Though not the ruler of Judea, Agrippa was well versed in Jewish affairs. Bernice was not Agrippa's wife, but his consort and sister. (Their sister, Drusilla, was married to the former governor, Felix). Their incestuous relationship was the talk of Rome, where Agrippa grew up. Bernice for a while became the mistress of Emperor Vespasian, then of his son, Titus, but always returned to her brother.

UNLEASHING THE TEXT

Read 21:17–26:32, noting the key words and definitions next to the passage.

the brethren received us gladly. (v. 17)—due to the much needed offering that had been brought as well as the presence of converted Gentiles with Paul

the elders (v. 18)—The apostles (away on evangelistic work) had turned over the rule of the Jerusalem church to a group of elders.

zealous for the law (v. 20)—These were not Judaizers, but believers who still observed the ceremonial aspects of the Mosaic Law.

Acts 21:17–26:32 (NKJV)

17 *And when we had come to Jerusalem, the brethren received us gladly.*

18 *On the following day Paul went in with us to James, and all the elders were present.*

19 *When he had greeted them, he told in detail those things which God had done among the Gentiles through his ministry.*

20 *And when they heard it, they glorified the Lord. And they said to him, "You see, brother, how many myriads of Jews there are who have believed, and they are all zealous for the law;*

21 *but they have been informed about you that you*

teach all the Jews who are among the Gentiles to forsake Moses, saying that they ought not to circumcise their children nor to walk according to the customs.

22 What then? The assembly must certainly meet, for they will hear that you have come.

23 Therefore do what we tell you: We have four men who have taken a vow.

24 Take them and be purified with them, and pay their expenses so that they may shave their heads, and that all may know that those things of which they were informed concerning you are nothing, but that you yourself also walk orderly and keep the law.

25 But concerning the Gentiles who believe, we have written and decided that they should observe no such thing, except that they should keep themselves from things offered to idols, from blood, from things strangled, and from sexual immorality."

26 Then Paul took the men, and the next day, having been purified with them, entered the temple to announce the expiration of the days of purification, at which time an offering should be made for each one of them.

27 Now when the seven days were almost ended, the Jews from Asia, seeing him in the temple, stirred up the whole crowd and laid hands on him,

28 crying out, "Men of Israel, help! This is the man who teaches all men everywhere against the people, the law, and this place; and furthermore he also brought Greeks into the temple and has defiled this holy place."

29 (For they had previously seen Trophimus the Ephesian with him in the city, whom they supposed that Paul had brought into the temple.)

30 And all the city was disturbed; and the people ran together, seized Paul, and dragged him out of the temple; and immediately the doors were shut.

31 Now as they were seeking to kill him, news came to the commander of the garrison that all Jerusalem was in an uproar.

to forsake Moses (v. 21)—The Judaizers made the false charge that Paul was teaching Jewish believers to turn their backs on their Jewish heritage (see 16:1–3 and 18:18 for evidence to the contrary); this lie was perpetuated and exaggerated shortly thereafter (see v. 28).

do what we tell you (v. 23)—James and the elders suggested that Paul undergo ritual purification at the temple to quell all the rumors.

seven days (v. 27)—the length of the purification process

Jews from Asia (v. 27)—likely Ephesus, since they recognized Trophimus as a Gentile (v. 29)

doors were shut (v. 30)—by the temple guards to prevent a murder from defiling the temple grounds

commander (v. 31)—This tribune was Claudius Lysias, the highest-ranking Roman in Jerusalem who commanded a force of a thousand men and was headquartered at Fort Antonia, located adjacent to the temple.

"Can you speak Greek?" (v. 37)—Paul's use of Greek (the language of the learned) startled the Roman commander; he assumed Paul was an uncultured Egyptian troublemaker (v. 38).

hear my defense (22:1)—the first of six recorded by Luke

Hebrew language (v. 2)— Aramaic, the language of Palestine

Gamaliel (v. 3)—That Paul had studied under such a celebrated rabbi was a serious blow to those who wanted to paint him as anti-law and anti-temple.

I persecuted this Way (v. 4)—Paul's former zeal for his Jewish heritage far outstripped the fervor of his accusers.

32 *He immediately took soldiers and centurions, and ran down to them. And when they saw the commander and the soldiers, they stopped beating Paul.*

33 *Then the commander came near and took him, and commanded him to be bound with two chains; and he asked who he was and what he had done.*

34 *And some among the multitude cried one thing and some another. So when he could not ascertain the truth because of the tumult, he commanded him to be taken into the barracks.*

35 *When he reached the stairs, he had to be carried by the soldiers because of the violence of the mob.*

36 *For the multitude of the people followed after, crying out, "Away with him!"*

37 *Then as Paul was about to be led into the barracks, he said to the commander, "May I speak to you?" He replied, "Can you speak Greek?*

38 *Are you not the Egyptian who some time ago stirred up a rebellion and led the four thousand assassins out into the wilderness?"*

39 *But Paul said, "I am a Jew from Tarsus, in Cilicia, a citizen of no mean city; and I implore you, permit me to speak to the people."*

40 *So when he had given him permission, Paul stood on the stairs and motioned with his hand to the people. And when there was a great silence, he spoke to them in the Hebrew language, saying,*

22:1 *"Brethren and fathers, hear my defense before you now."*

2 *And when they heard that he spoke to them in the Hebrew language, they kept all the more silent. Then he said:*

3 *"I am indeed a Jew, born in Tarsus of Cilicia, but brought up in this city at the feet of Gamaliel, taught according to the strictness of our fathers' law, and was zealous toward God as you all are today.*

4 *I persecuted this Way to the death, binding and delivering into prisons both men and women,*

5 *as also the high priest bears me witness, and all the council of the elders, from whom I also received*

letters to the brethren, and went to Damascus to bring in chains even those who were there to Jerusalem to be punished.

6 "Now it happened, as I journeyed and came near Damascus at about noon, suddenly a great light from heaven shone around me.

7 And I fell to the ground and heard a voice saying to me, 'Saul, Saul, why are you persecuting Me?'

8 So I answered, 'Who are You, Lord?' And He said to me, 'I am Jesus of Nazareth, whom you are persecuting.'

9 "And those who were with me indeed saw the light and were afraid, but they did not hear the voice of Him who spoke to me.

10 So I said, 'What shall I do, Lord?' And the Lord said to me, 'Arise and go into Damascus, and there you will be told all things which are appointed for you to do.'

11 And since I could not see for the glory of that light, being led by the hand of those who were with me, I came into Damascus.

12 "Then a certain Ananias, a devout man according to the law, having a good testimony with all the Jews who dwelt there,

13 came to me; and he stood and said to me, 'Brother Saul, receive your sight.' And at that same hour I looked up at him.

14 Then he said, 'The God of our fathers has chosen you that you should know His will, and see the Just One, and hear the voice of His mouth.

15 For you will be His witness to all men of what you have seen and heard.

16 And now why are you waiting? Arise and be baptized, and wash away your sins, calling on the name of the Lord.'

17 "Now it happened, when I returned to Jerusalem and was praying in the temple, that I was in a trance

18 and saw Him saying to me, 'Make haste and get out of Jerusalem quickly, for they will not receive your testimony concerning Me.'

wash away your sins (v. 16)— Grammatically the phrase "calling on the name of the Lord," precedes "arise and be baptized." Salvation comes from calling on the name of the Lord (Rom. 10:9, 10, 13), not from being baptized.

19 *So I said, 'Lord, they know that in every synagogue I imprisoned and beat those who believe on You.*

20 *And when the blood of Your martyr Stephen was shed, I also was standing by consenting to his death, and guarding the clothes of those who were killing him.'*

21 *Then He said to me, 'Depart, for I will send you far from here to the Gentiles.' "*

22 *And they listened to him until this word, and then they raised their voices and said, "Away with such a fellow from the earth, for he is not fit to live!"*

23 *Then, as they cried out and tore off their clothes and threw dust into the air,*

24 *the commander ordered him to be brought into the barracks, and said that he should be examined under scourging, so that he might know why they shouted so against him.*

25 *And as they bound him with thongs, Paul said to the centurion who stood by, "Is it lawful for you to scourge a man who is a Roman, and uncondemned?"*

26 *When the centurion heard that, he went and told the commander, saying, "Take care what you do, for this man is a Roman."*

27 *Then the commander came and said to him, "Tell me, are you a Roman?" He said, "Yes."*

28 *The commander answered, "With a large sum I obtained this citizenship." And Paul said, "But I was born a citizen."*

29 *Then immediately those who were about to examine him withdrew from him; and the commander was also afraid after he found out that he was a Roman, and because he had bound him.*

30 *The next day, because he wanted to know for certain why he was accused by the Jews, he released him from his bonds, and commanded the chief priests and all their council to appear, and brought Paul down and set him before them.*

23:1 *Then Paul, looking earnestly at the council, said, "Men and brethren, I have lived in all good conscience before God until this day."*

2 And the high priest Ananias commanded those who stood by him to strike him on the mouth.

3 Then Paul said to him, "God will strike you, you whitewashed wall! For you sit to judge me according to the law, and do you command me to be struck contrary to the law?"

4 And those who stood by said, "Do you revile God's high priest?"

5 Then Paul said, "I did not know, brethren, that he was the high priest; for it is written, 'You shall not speak evil of a ruler of your people.'"

6 But when Paul perceived that one part were Sadducees and the other Pharisees, he cried out in the council, "Men and brethren, I am a Pharisee, the son of a Pharisee; concerning the hope and resurrection of the dead I am being judged!"

7 And when he had said this, a dissension arose between the Pharisees and the Sadducees; and the assembly was divided.

8 For Sadducees say that there is no resurrection—and no angel or spirit; but the Pharisees confess both.

9 Then there arose a loud outcry. And the scribes of the Pharisees' party arose and protested, saying, "We find no evil in this man; but if a spirit or an angel has spoken to him, let us not fight against God."

10 Now when there arose a great dissension, the commander, fearing lest Paul might be pulled to pieces by them, commanded the soldiers to go down and take him by force from among them, and bring him into the barracks.

11 But the following night the Lord stood by him and said, "Be of good cheer, Paul; for as you have testified for Me in Jerusalem, so you must also bear witness at Rome."

12 And when it was day, some of the Jews banded together and bound themselves under an oath, saying that they would neither eat nor drink till they had killed Paul.

Ananias (23:2)—one of Israel's cruelest and most corrupt high priests; his illegal command for Paul to be struck was in keeping with his evil character

you whitewashed wall (v. 3)—Paul reacted angrily and spoke derisively to Ananias; he later admitted he had violated God's express prohibition against slandering a ruler, quoting Exodus 22:28, and explained that he didn't know his accuser was the high priest—a statement most attribute to sarcasm or offer as proof of Paul's poor eyesight.

a dissension arose (v. 7)—The issue of the resurrection was perhaps the biggest theological hot potato between the Pharisees and Sadducees; the Sadducees accepted only the Pentateuch, which does not overtly teach the doctrine of the resurrection.

the Lord stood by him (v. 11)—the fifth of six visions recorded by Luke; in this one the Lord assured Paul of eventual arrival in Rome

bound themselves under an oath (v. 12)—Essentially they invoked divine judgment if they did not carry out their plot.

13 Now there were more than forty who had formed this conspiracy.

14 They came to the chief priests and elders, and said, "We have bound ourselves under a great oath that we will eat nothing until we have killed Paul.

15 Now you, therefore, together with the council, suggest to the commander that he be brought down to you tomorrow, as though you were going to make further inquiries concerning him; but we are ready to kill him before he comes near."

16 So when Paul's sister's son heard of their ambush, he went and entered the barracks and told Paul.

Paul's sister's son (v. 16)—the only clear reference in the New Testament to Paul's family; this nephew somehow learned of the Jewish plot and was able to warn his uncle

17 Then Paul called one of the centurions to him and said, "Take this young man to the commander, for he has something to tell him."

18 So he took him and brought him to the commander and said, "Paul the prisoner called me to him and asked me to bring this young man to you. He has something to say to you."

19 Then the commander took him by the hand, went aside, and asked privately, "What is it that you have to tell me?"

20 And he said, "The Jews have agreed to ask that you bring Paul down to the council tomorrow, as though they were going to inquire more fully about him.

21 But do not yield to them, for more than forty of them lie in wait for him, men who have bound themselves by an oath that they will neither eat nor drink till they have killed him; and now they are ready, waiting for the promise from you."

22 So the commander let the young man depart, and commanded him, "Tell no one that you have revealed these things to me."

23 And he called for two centurions, saying, "Prepare two hundred soldiers, seventy horsemen, and two hundred spearmen to go to Caesarea at the third hour of the night;

bring him safely to Felix (v. 24)—Lysias regarded the Jewish threat as serious enough to warrant Paul's removal to Caesarea; a contingent of almost five hundred men were assigned to protect the apostle.

24 and provide mounts to set Paul on, and bring him safely to Felix the governor."

25 He wrote a letter in the following manner:

26 Claudius Lysias, To the most excellent governor Felix: Greetings.

27 This man was seized by the Jews and was about to be killed by them. Coming with the troops I rescued him, having learned that he was a Roman.

28 And when I wanted to know the reason they accused him, I brought him before their council.

29 I found out that he was accused concerning questions of their law, but had nothing charged against him deserving of death or chains.

30 And when it was told me that the Jews lay in wait for the man, I sent him immediately to you, and also commanded his accusers to state before you the charges against him. Farewell.

31 Then the soldiers, as they were commanded, took Paul and brought him by night to Antipatris.

32 The next day they left the horsemen to go on with him, and returned to the barracks.

33 When they came to Caesarea and had delivered the letter to the governor, they also presented Paul to him.

34 And when the governor had read it, he asked what province he was from. And when he understood that he was from Cilicia,

35 he said, "I will hear you when your accusers also have come." And he commanded him to be kept in Herod's Praetorium.

24:1 Now after five days Ananias the high priest came down with the elders and a certain orator named Tertullus. These gave evidence to the governor against Paul.

2 And when he was called upon, Tertullus began his accusation, saying: "Seeing that through you we enjoy great peace, and prosperity is being brought to this nation by your foresight,

3 we accept it always and in all places, most noble Felix, with all thankfulness.

4 Nevertheless, not to be tedious to you any further, I

concerning questions of their law (v. 29)—Lysias wrote this letter to Felix, painting himself in the best possible light and making no mention of any crimes against Roman law—in essence, declaring Paul innocent.

Herod's Praetorium (v. 35)—Felix's official residence in Caesarea

Tertullus began (24:2)—Tertullus may have been a Roman; more likely he was a Hellenistic Jew. His opening statement accuses Paul of sedition (a crime against Roman law), sectarianism (a violation of Jewish law), and sacrilege (a violation of divine law).

Felix (v. 3)—the brutal and largely ineffective governor of Judea from AD 52 to 59

beg you to hear, by your courtesy, a few words from us.

5 For we have found this man a plague, a creator of dissension among all the Jews throughout the world, and a ringleader of the sect of the Nazarenes.

6 He even tried to profane the temple, and we seized him, and wanted to judge him according to our law.

7 But the commander Lysias came by and with great violence took him out of our hands,

8 commanding his accusers to come to you. By examining him yourself you may ascertain all these things of which we accuse him."

9 And the Jews also assented, maintaining that these things were so.

10 Then Paul, after the governor had nodded to him to speak, answered: "Inasmuch as I know that you have been for many years a judge of this nation, I do the more cheerfully answer for myself,

11 because you may ascertain that it is no more than twelve days since I went up to Jerusalem to worship.

12 And they neither found me in the temple disputing with anyone nor inciting the crowd, either in the synagogues or in the city.

13 Nor can they prove the things of which they now accuse me.

14 But this I confess to you, that according to the Way which they call a sect, so I worship the God of my fathers, believing all things which are written in the Law and in the Prophets.

15 I have hope in God, which they themselves also accept, that there will be a resurrection of the dead, both of the just and the unjust.

16 This being so, I myself always strive to have a conscience without offense toward God and men.

17 "Now after many years I came to bring alms and offerings to my nation,

18 in the midst of which some Jews from Asia found me purified in the temple, neither with a mob nor with tumult.

Then Paul . . . answered (v. 10)—the third of Paul's six defenses recorded in Acts; here he reiterated the facts surrounding his arrest and essentially argued that he was standing before Felix for no other reason than his belief in the resurrection of the dead (that is, theological beliefs rather than criminal acts)

19 They ought to have been here before you to object if they had anything against me.

20 Or else let those who are here themselves say if they found any wrongdoing in me while I stood before the council,

21 unless it is for this one statement which I cried out, standing among them, 'Concerning the resurrection of the dead I am being judged by you this day.' "

22 But when Felix heard these things, having more accurate knowledge of the Way, he adjourned the proceedings and said, "When Lysias the commander comes down, I will make a decision on your case."

23 So he commanded the centurion to keep Paul and to let him have liberty, and told him not to forbid any of his friends to provide for or visit him.

24 And after some days, when Felix came with his wife Drusilla, who was Jewish, he sent for Paul and heard him concerning the faith in Christ.

25 Now as he reasoned about righteousness, self-control, and the judgment to come, Felix was afraid and answered, "Go away for now; when I have a convenient time I will call for you."

26 Meanwhile he also hoped that money would be given him by Paul, that he might release him. Therefore he sent for him more often and conversed with him.

27 But after two years Porcius Festus succeeded Felix; and Felix, wanting to do the Jews a favor, left Paul bound.

25:1 Now when Festus had come to the province, after three days he went up from Caesarea to Jerusalem.

2 Then the high priest and the chief men of the Jews informed him against Paul; and they petitioned him,

3 asking a favor against him, that he would summon him to Jerusalem—while they lay in ambush along the road to kill him.

4 But Festus answered that Paul should be kept at Caesarea, and that he himself was going there shortly.

having more accurate knowledge of the Way (v. 22)—probably from his wife Drusilla, who was Jewish (25:24)

adjourned the proceedings (v. 22)—Since Paul's original accusers (that is, the Jews from Asia) had not appeared, no compelling case had been made by Tertullus, and a "not guilty" verdict would upset the peace, Felix reasoned that the best decision was no decision.

heard him concerning the faith in Christ (v. 24)—A private audience with Paul, who spoke bluntly about the things of God, left Felix afraid—he was involved in a sinful relationship with Drusilla, a woman he had lured away from her husband.

ambush (25:3)—a second murderous plot instigated after Porcius Festus succeeded Felix

121

5   "Therefore," he said, "let those who have authority
    among you go down with me and accuse this man,
    to see if there is any fault in him."

6   And when he had remained among them more than
    ten days, he went down to Caesarea. And the next
    day, sitting on the judgment seat, he commanded
    Paul to be brought.

7   When he had come, the Jews who had come down
    from Jerusalem stood about and laid many serious
    complaints against Paul, which they could not prove,

8   while he answered for himself, "Neither against the
    law of the Jews, nor against the temple, nor against
    Caesar have I offended in anything at all."

9   But Festus, wanting to do the Jews a favor, answered
    Paul and said, "Are you willing to go up to
    Jerusalem and there be judged before me concerning
    these things?"

10 So Paul said, "I stand at Caesar's judgment seat,
    where I ought to be judged. To the Jews I have done
    no wrong, as you very well know.

11 For if I am an offender, or have committed anything
    deserving of death, I do not object to dying; but if
    there is nothing in these things of which these men
    accuse me, no one can deliver me to them. I appeal
    to Caesar."

12 Then Festus, when he had conferred with the
    council, answered, "You have appealed to Caesar?
    To Caesar you shall go!"

13 And after some days King Agrippa and Bernice
    came to Caesarea to greet Festus.

14 When they had been there many days, Festus laid
    Paul's case before the king, saying: "There is a
    certain man left a prisoner by Felix,

15 about whom the chief priests and the elders of the
    Jews informed me, when I was in Jerusalem, asking
    for a judgment against him.

16 To them I answered, 'It is not the custom of the
    Romans to deliver any man to destruction before
    the accused meets the accusers face to face, and has

opportunity to answer for himself concerning the charge against him.'

17 *Therefore when they had come together, without any delay, the next day I sat on the judgment seat and commanded the man to be brought in.*

18 *When the accusers stood up, they brought no accusation against him of such things as I supposed,*

19 *but had some questions against him about their own religion and about a certain Jesus, who had died, whom Paul affirmed to be alive.*

20 *And because I was uncertain of such questions, I asked whether he was willing to go to Jerusalem and there be judged concerning these matters.*

21 *But when Paul appealed to be reserved for the decision of Augustus, I commanded him to be kept till I could send him to Caesar."*

22 *Then Agrippa said to Festus, "I also would like to hear the man myself." "Tomorrow," he said, "you shall hear him."*

23 *So the next day, when Agrippa and Bernice had come with great pomp, and had entered the auditorium with the commanders and the prominent men of the city, at Festus' command Paul was brought in.*

24 *And Festus said: "King Agrippa and all the men who are here present with us, you see this man about whom the whole assembly of the Jews petitioned me, both at Jerusalem and here, crying out that he was not fit to live any longer.*

25 *But when I found that he had committed nothing deserving of death, and that he himself had appealed to Augustus, I decided to send him.*

26 *I have nothing certain to write to my lord concerning him. Therefore I have brought him out before you, and especially before you, King Agrippa, so that after the examination has taken place I may have something to write.*

27 *For it seems to me unreasonable to send a prisoner and not to specify the charges against him."*

I was uncertain (v. 20)—Festus was a pagan Roman who knew that the charges against Paul involved religious, not civil, matters about which he knew very little.

I also would like to hear (v. 22)—The Greek verb tense suggests that Herod had been wanting to hear Paul for some time; as an expert on Jewish affairs, he relished hearing Christianity's leading spokesman. This pleased Festus, who needed help in outlining the charges against Paul in his official report for Nero.

stretched out his hand (26:1)—
a common gesture at the beginning of an address

26:1 *Then Agrippa said to Paul, "You are permitted to
speak for yourself." So Paul stretched out his hand
and answered for himself:*

2 *"I think myself happy, King Agrippa, because today I
shall answer for myself before you concerning all the
things of which I am accused by the Jews,*

3 *especially because you are expert in all customs and
questions which have to do with the Jews. Therefore
I beg you to hear me patiently.*

4 *"My manner of life from my youth, which was
spent from the beginning among my own nation at
Jerusalem, all the Jews know.*

5 *They knew me from the first, if they were willing
to testify, that according to the strictest sect of our
religion I lived a Pharisee.*

6 *And now I stand and am judged for the hope of the
promise made by God to our fathers.*

7 *To this promise our twelve tribes, earnestly serving
God night and day, hope to attain. For this hope's
sake, King Agrippa, I am accused by the Jews.*

8 *Why should it be thought incredible by you that
God raises the dead?*

9 *"Indeed, I myself thought I must do many things
contrary to the name of Jesus of Nazareth.*

10 *This I also did in Jerusalem, and many of the saints
I shut up in prison, having received authority from
the chief priests; and when they were put to death, I
cast my vote against them.*

11 *And I punished them often in every synagogue
and compelled them to blaspheme; and being
exceedingly enraged against them, I persecuted
them even to foreign cities.*

12 *"While thus occupied, as I journeyed to Damascus
with authority and commission from the chief priests,*

13 *at midday, O king, along the road I saw a light from
heaven, brighter than the sun, shining around me
and those who journeyed with me.*

14 *And when we all had fallen to the ground, I heard
a voice speaking to me and saying in the Hebrew*

I cast my vote (v. 10)—literally,
"I threw my pebble"—a reference to the ancient practice of
recording votes by means of
small colored stones; this may
indicate Paul was a member of
the Sanhedrin

124

language, 'Saul, Saul, why are you persecuting Me? It is hard for you to kick against the goads.'

15 So I said, 'Who are You, Lord?' And He said, 'I am Jesus, whom you are persecuting.

16 But rise and stand on your feet; for I have appeared to you for this purpose, to make you a minister and a witness both of the things which you have seen and of the things which I will yet reveal to you.

17 I will deliver you from the Jewish people, as well as from the Gentiles, to whom I now send you,

18 to open their eyes, in order to turn them from darkness to light, and from the power of Satan to God, that they may receive forgiveness of sins and an inheritance among those who are sanctified by faith in Me.'

19 "Therefore, King Agrippa, I was not disobedient to the heavenly vision,

20 but declared first to those in Damascus and in Jerusalem, and throughout all the region of Judea, and then to the Gentiles, that they should repent, turn to God, and do works befitting repentance.

works befitting repentance (v. 20)—Genuine repentance is inseparably linked to a changed lifestyle.

21 For these reasons the Jews seized me in the temple and tried to kill me.

22 Therefore, having obtained help from God, to this day I stand, witnessing both to small and great, saying no other things than those which the prophets and Moses said would come—

23 that the Christ would suffer, that He would be the first to rise from the dead, and would proclaim light to the Jewish people and to the Gentiles."

24 Now as he thus made his defense, Festus said with a loud voice, "Paul, you are beside yourself! Much learning is driving you mad!"

you are beside yourself! (v. 24)—Shocked that an obviously learned man like Paul could actually believe that the dead can live again, Festus accused Paul of being insane.

25 But he said, "I am not mad, most noble Festus, but speak the words of truth and reason.

26 For the king, before whom I also speak freely, knows these things; for I am convinced that none of these things escapes his attention, since this thing was not done in a corner.

not done in a corner (v. 26)—Paul asserted that Christ's life and works were common knowledge in Palestine.

do you believe the prophets? (v. 27)—This shrewd question put Agrippa in a bind, for if he said yes, he would have to agree with Paul's statements and look foolish in the eyes of the Romans. If he said no, he would outrage his Jewish subjects.

You almost persuade me (v. 28)—The idea is, "Do you think you can convince me to become a Christian in such a short time?" Agrippa evaded Paul's pointed inquiry.

27 *King Agrippa, do you believe the prophets? I know that you do believe."*

28 *Then Agrippa said to Paul, "You almost persuade me to become a Christian."*

29 *And Paul said, "I would to God that not only you, but also all who hear me today, might become both almost and altogether such as I am, except for these chains."*

30 *When he had said these things, the king stood up, as well as the governor and Bernice and those who sat with them;*

31 *and when they had gone aside, they talked among themselves, saying, "This man is doing nothing deserving of death or chains."*

32 *Then Agrippa said to Festus, "This man might have been set free if he had not appealed to Caesar."*

1) What happened when Paul got to Jerusalem and went to the temple to undergo ritual purification (21:17–26)? Why did Paul feel the need to submit to this Jewish rite?

_____

_____

_____

_____

2) How did Paul's Roman citizenship end up being a tremendous blessing (21:37; 22:25; 23:27–29)?

_____

_____

_____

3) What were some of his other qualities and credentials that enhanced his ability to relate to Jewish and Gentile alike (21:37–39; 22:1–5; 24:24–25; 26:1–3)?

_____

_____

_____

4) What subject caused an uproar during Paul's address to the Sanhedrin (22:20–24)? Why? What two factions in the Jewish council began bickering (23:6–10)?

_____

_____

_____

_____

Going Deeper

Paul was tried before the Jewish rulers and the Roman rulers, as Jesus was. Read Matthew 26:57–65 and 27:11–14 to find out more about Jesus' trials.

Exploring the Meaning

5) How did Jesus' response to questioning compare and contrast with Paul's responses? Why do you think Jesus responded as He did?

_____

_____

_____

_____

6) The Jews were filled with a murderous hatred toward Paul. They engaged in several concerted and intense efforts to kill him but failed. What does this say about the purposes of God? About the people's evil intent?

_____

_____

_____

7) On more than one occasion, Paul utilized his privileges and protections as a Roman citizen to avoid certain harm. What principle(s) do you see for us today? When do you think we should submit and suffer quietly? When should we insist on our rights?

_____

_____

_____

Truth for Today

Paul used his circumstances as an opportunity. The crowd (21:30–31) had not gathered to hear him preach but to beat and kill him. Paul, however, used that occasion to proclaim to them how God's saving power had transformed his life.

Reflecting on the Text

8) In what negative situations in your life might you be able to shine for Christ? How?

_____

_____

_____

9) What practical and helpful principles of evangelism can we glean from Paul's experiences in these chapters?

_____

_____

_____

10) Re-read 26:18. How can you properly express your gratitude this week to God for the wonderful gift of salvation?

_____

_____

_____

Personal Response

Write out additional reflections, questions you may have, or a prayer.

_____

_____

_____

_____

_____

_____

~ 12 ~
THE TRIUMPH OF THE GOSPEL

Acts 27:1–28:31

DRAWING NEAR

Paul suffered a great deal but he always trusted that God was working for good. Do you have confidence that God is in control of your life? Why or why not?

_____

_____

_____

THE CONTEXT

Paul's longtime dream was finally reached in these final two chapters. At long last, Paul boarded a boat for Rome, probably in October (AD 59). He was accompanied, at the very least, by Luke (the first person plural pronoun "we" opens this section) and Aristarchus. This was late in the fall to be on the open seas. Sure enough, bad weather made for rough sailing. Paul sensed real danger ahead and encouraged the crew to find safe harbor for the winter. Nevertheless, the leaders of the voyage pressed on, providing a fitting sense of drama near the end of Luke's masterful history of the early church.

At the height of a violent storm, Paul gathered the ship's crew and encouraged them with the promises of God: (1) that he had been guaranteed safe arrival in Rome; (2) that everyone sailing with him would be protected from harm. Even so, a shipwreck was inevitable. In time, the ship ran aground and began to break apart just off the coast of Malta. Though the experience proved to be harrowing, all 276 people on board were able to swim safely ashore.

On the island of Malta, the forces of hell continued their all-out attempt to keep God's messenger from reaching Rome. Here Paul was bitten by a poisonous snake. Paul not only survived the serpent's attack unharmed, but he also healed a number of sick people on the island. During the three-month stay in Malta (see 28:11), Paul was showered with hospitality. What the Enemy intended for evil, God turned into good.

Reaching Italy, Paul was warmly received by some Italian believers, and he was granted his own private lodging (that is, house arrest rather than imprisonment in a Roman penal facility). The stage was now set for Paul to begin ministering in the most influential city in the world.

KEYS TO THE TEXT

Rome: The capital city of the Roman Empire. The apostle Paul's first known connection with Rome was when he met Aquila and Priscilla at Corinth (Acts 18:2). They had left Rome when Claudius expelled all the Jews from the city. Some few years after meeting Aquila and Priscilla, Paul decided that he "must also see Rome." When he wrote his letter to the Christians at Rome, his plan was to visit friends in the city on his way to Spain. However, Paul actually went to Rome under very different conditions than he had originally planned. To keep from being killed by hostile Jews in Jerusalem, Paul appealed to Caesar. The binding effect of that appeal ultimately brought him to the capital city as a prisoner. Here he waited for his trial.

The city to which Paul came was very similar to a modern city. The public buildings and other structures were lavishly constructed. In AD 28 Augustus built a great temple to Apollo near his palace on the Palatine Hill. A new senate house and a temple to honor Caesar had been constructed in AD 29, as well as other buildings, including the Colosseum where the Roman chariot races and gladiatorial contests occurred. The houses of the wealthy people of Rome were elaborately constructed. But over a million people lived in crowded tenement dwellings that engulfed the city. The city of Rome became a symbol of paganism and idolatry in the New Testament.

UNLEASHING THE TEXT

Read 27:1–28:31, noting the key words and definitions next to the passage.

we (v. 1)—Luke rejoined Paul, ostensibly to care for him on his voyage and during his Roman imprisonment.

Adramyttium (v. 2)—a city on the northwest coast of Asia Minor (modern Turkey) where the centurion hoped to find a ship headed for Rome

Aristarchus (v. 2)—the man seized by the crowd during the riot at Ephesus (see 19:29); he would be with Paul during the apostle's first Roman imprisonment

landed at Sidon (v. 3)—The Christians here ministered to Paul, possibly by providing provisions for his voyage.

Acts 27:1–28:31 (NKJV)

1 *And when it was decided that we should sail to Italy, they delivered Paul and some other prisoners to one named Julius, a centurion of the Augustan Regiment.*

2 *So, entering a ship of Adramyttium, we put to sea, meaning to sail along the coasts of Asia. Aristarchus, a Macedonian of Thessalonica, was with us.*

3 *And the next day we landed at Sidon. And Julius treated Paul kindly and gave him liberty to go to his friends and receive care.*

4 *When we had put to sea from there, we sailed under the shelter of Cyprus, because the winds were contrary.*

5 *And when we had sailed over the sea which is off Cilicia and Pamphylia, we came to Myra, a city of Lycia.*

6 *There the centurion found an Alexandrian ship sailing to Italy, and he put us on board.*

7 When we had sailed slowly many days, and arrived with difficulty off Cnidus, the wind not permitting us to proceed, we sailed under the shelter of Crete off Salmone.

8 Passing it with difficulty, we came to a place called Fair Havens, near the city of Lasea.

9 Now when much time had been spent, and sailing was now dangerous because the Fast was already over, Paul advised them,

10 saying, "Men, I perceive that this voyage will end with disaster and much loss, not only of the cargo and ship, but also our lives."

11 Nevertheless the centurion was more persuaded by the helmsman and the owner of the ship than by the things spoken by Paul.

12 And because the harbor was not suitable to winter in, the majority advised to set sail from there also, if by any means they could reach Phoenix, a harbor of Crete opening toward the southwest and northwest, and winter there.

13 When the south wind blew softly, supposing that they had obtained their desire, putting out to sea, they sailed close by Crete.

14 But not long after, a tempestuous head wind arose, called Euroclydon.

15 So when the ship was caught, and could not head into the wind, we let her drive.

16 And running under the shelter of an island called Clauda, we secured the skiff with difficulty.

17 When they had taken it on board, they used cables to undergird the ship; and fearing lest they should run aground on the Syrtis Sands, they struck sail and so were driven.

18 And because we were exceedingly tempest-tossed, the next day they lightened the ship.

19 On the third day we threw the ship's tackle overboard with our own hands.

20 Now when neither sun nor stars appeared for many days, and no small tempest beat on us, all hope that we would be saved was finally given up.

---

sailed under the shelter of Cyprus (v. 4)—that is, they stayed between it and the mainland rather than venture out into the open seas

Alexandrian ship (v. 6)—part of the imperial grain fleet

Cnidus (v. 7)—on a peninsula in extreme southwest Asia Minor; here the headwinds became too strong to continue west

the Fast was already over (v. 9)—The Day of Atonement (late September or early October) had come and gone, meaning that the optimal time for sea travel had passed.

end with disaster (v. 10)—Paul advised wintering at Fair Havens to avoid trouble at sea.

centurion (v. 11)—Because the ship was part of the imperial grain fleet, Julius (see v. 1), not the helmsman or the ship's owner, was the ranking official.

Phoenix (v. 12)—The sailors considered this a better harbor than Fair Havens.

Euroclydon (v. 14)—Euraquilon is the preferred reading; the word refers to a strong, dangerous windstorm greatly feared even by experienced sailors in the Mediterranean.

secured the skiff (v. 16)—They brought the dinghy on board.

used cables (v. 17)—Known also as "frapping," this practice helped hold the ship together.

lightened the ship (v. 18)—throwing all unnecessary gear and cargo overboard to lighten the ship and help it ride the rough waves

stood by me this night an angel (v. 23)—the last of Paul's six visions recorded in Acts

before Caesar (v. 24)—a reaffirmation of the promise Jesus had made earlier to Paul (see 23:11)

sensed (v. 27)—The sailors probably heard the sound of the waves breaking on the shore.

took soundings (v. 28)—using a weight attached to a length of rope; the decreasing measurements confirmed they were nearing land

putting out anchors from the prow (v. 30)—a common practice for additional stability

without food (v. 33)—due, likely, to the conditions and perhaps also to seasickness in the rough waters

not a hair will fall (v. 34)—a common Jewish saying (see 2 Sam. 14:11; 1 Kin. 1:52; Luke 21:18)

21 But after long abstinence from food, then Paul stood in the midst of them and said, "Men, you should have listened to me, and not have sailed from Crete and incurred this disaster and loss.

22 And now I urge you to take heart, for there will be no loss of life among you, but only of the ship.

23 For there stood by me this night an angel of the God to whom I belong and whom I serve,

24 saying, 'Do not be afraid, Paul; you must be brought before Caesar; and indeed God has granted you all those who sail with you.'

25 Therefore take heart, men, for I believe God that it will be just as it was told me.

26 However, we must run aground on a certain island."

27 Now when the fourteenth night had come, as we were driven up and down in the Adriatic Sea, about midnight the sailors sensed that they were drawing near some land.

28 And they took soundings and found it to be twenty fathoms; and when they had gone a little farther, they took soundings again and found it to be fifteen fathoms.

29 Then, fearing lest we should run aground on the rocks, they dropped four anchors from the stern, and prayed for day to come.

30 And as the sailors were seeking to escape from the ship, when they had let down the skiff into the sea, under pretense of putting out anchors from the prow,

31 Paul said to the centurion and the soldiers, "Unless these men stay in the ship, you cannot be saved."

32 Then the soldiers cut away the ropes of the skiff and let it fall off.

33 And as day was about to dawn, Paul implored them all to take food, saying, "Today is the fourteenth day you have waited and continued without food, and eaten nothing.

34 Therefore I urge you to take nourishment, for this is for your survival, since not a hair will fall from the head of any of you."

35 And when he had said these things, he took bread

and gave thanks to God in the presence of them all; and when he had broken it he began to eat.

36 Then they were all encouraged, and also took food themselves.

37 And in all we were two hundred and seventy-six persons on the ship.

38 So when they had eaten enough, they lightened the ship and threw out the wheat into the sea.

39 When it was day, they did not recognize the land; but they observed a bay with a beach, onto which they planned to run the ship if possible.

40 And they let go the anchors and left them in the sea, meanwhile loosing the rudder ropes; and they hoisted the mainsail to the wind and made for shore.

41 But striking a place where two seas met, they ran the ship aground; and the prow stuck fast and remained immovable, but the stern was being broken up by the violence of the waves.

a place where two seas met (v. 41)—a sandbar or reef

42 And the soldiers' plan was to kill the prisoners, lest any of them should swim away and escape.

kill the prisoners (v. 42)—to protect themselves from punishment lest one or more prisoners escape

43 But the centurion, wanting to save Paul, kept them from their purpose, and commanded that those who could swim should jump overboard first and get to land,

44 and the rest, some on boards and some on parts of the ship. And so it was that they all escaped safely to land.

28:1 Now when they had escaped, they then found out that the island was called Malta.

2 And the natives showed us unusual kindness; for they kindled a fire and made us all welcome, because of the rain that was falling and because of the cold.

3 But when Paul had gathered a bundle of sticks and laid them on the fire, a viper came out because of the heat, and fastened on his hand.

a viper (28:3)—a venomous snake

4 So when the natives saw the creature hanging from his hand, they said to one another, "No doubt this man is a murderer, whom, though he has escaped the sea, yet justice does not allow to live."

5 But he shook off the creature into the fire and suffered no harm.

leading citizen (v. 7)—Publius was governor of Malta.

sick of a fever (v. 8)—Gastric fever (caused by a microbe in goat's milk) was common on the island.

Twin Brothers (v. 11)—Castor and Pollux, Zeus' sons according to Greek mythology, were believed to provide special protection to sailors.

Rhegium (v. 13)—a harbor on the southern tip of the Italian mainland

dwell by himself . . . guarded (v. 16)—Paul, possibly through Julius' intervention, was allowed to live under guard in his own rented quarters.

the customs of our fathers (v. 17)—Paul denied that he was guilty of the charges against him—that is, that he had violated Jewish laws or customs.

6 *However, they were expecting that he would swell up or suddenly fall down dead. But after they had looked for a long time and saw no harm come to him, they changed their minds and said that he was a god.*

7 *In that region there was an estate of the leading citizen of the island, whose name was Publius, who received us and entertained us courteously for three days.*

8 *And it happened that the father of Publius lay sick of a fever and dysentery. Paul went in to him and prayed, and he laid his hands on him and healed him.*

9 *So when this was done, the rest of those on the island who had diseases also came and were healed.*

10 *They also honored us in many ways; and when we departed, they provided such things as were necessary.*

11 *After three months we sailed in an Alexandrian ship whose figurehead was the Twin Brothers, which had wintered at the island.*

12 *And landing at Syracuse, we stayed three days.*

13 *From there we circled round and reached Rhegium. And after one day the south wind blew; and the next day we came to Puteoli,*

14 *where we found brethren, and were invited to stay with them seven days. And so we went toward Rome.*

15 *And from there, when the brethren heard about us, they came to meet us as far as Appii Forum and Three Inns. When Paul saw them, he thanked God and took courage.*

16 *Now when we came to Rome, the centurion delivered the prisoners to the captain of the guard; but Paul was permitted to dwell by himself with the soldier who guarded him.*

17 *And it came to pass after three days that Paul called the leaders of the Jews together. So when they had come together, he said to them: "Men and brethren, though I have done nothing against our people or the customs of our fathers, yet I was delivered as a prisoner from Jerusalem into the hands of the Romans,*

18 *who, when they had examined me, wanted to let me go, because there was no cause for putting me to death.*

19 *But when the Jews spoke against it, I was compelled to appeal to Caesar, not that I had anything of which to accuse my nation.*

20 *For this reason therefore I have called for you, to see you and speak with you, because for the hope of Israel I am bound with this chain."*

21 *Then they said to him, "We neither received letters from Judea concerning you, nor have any of the brethren who came reported or spoken any evil of you.*

22 *But we desire to hear from you what you think; for concerning this sect, we know that it is spoken against everywhere."*

23 *So when they had appointed him a day, many came to him at his lodging, to whom he explained and solemnly testified of the kingdom of God, persuading them concerning Jesus from both the Law of Moses and the Prophets, from morning till evening.*

persuading them . . . Law of Moses . . . Prophets (v. 23)— Paul's method of Jewish evangelism was to show from the Old Testament that Jesus is the Messiah.

24 *And some were persuaded by the things which were spoken, and some disbelieved.*

25 *So when they did not agree among themselves, they departed after Paul had said one word: "The Holy Spirit spoke rightly through Isaiah the prophet to our fathers,*

26 *saying, 'Go to this people and say: "Hearing you will hear, and shall not understand; And seeing you will see, and not perceive;*

27 *For the hearts of this people have grown dull. Their ears are hard of hearing, And their eyes they have closed, Lest they should see with their eyes and hear with their ears, Lest they should understand with their hearts and turn, So that I should heal them." '*

28 *"Therefore let it be known to you that the salvation of God has been sent to the Gentiles, and they will hear it!"*

29 *And when he had said these words, the Jews departed and had a great dispute among themselves.*

30 *Then Paul dwelt two whole years in his own rented house, and received all who came to him,*

31 *preaching the kingdom of God and teaching the things which concern the Lord Jesus Christ with all confidence, no one forbidding him.*

preaching the kingdom . . . no one forbidding him (v. 31)— Paul evangelized Rome with the help of his loyal fellow workers.

1) In what ways was the voyage to Rome described in chapter 27 as an ill-advised decision?

_____

_____

_____

_____

2) How did Paul demonstrate the qualities of a leader during the harrowing voyage to Rome?

_____

_____

_____

_____

3) What happened when Paul arrived at Rome?

_____

_____

_____

_____

GOING DEEPER

While Paul awaited trial, he was busy writing encouragement and instructions to the new churches. Read Philippians 2:1–16 for some of what Paul wrote.

EXPLORING THE MEANING

4) What incidents in Acts 27 and 28 demonstrate that Paul practiced what he preached in Philippians 2—that is, that he considered others as more important than himself?

_____

_____

_____

_____

5) Read 2 Timothy 4:1–5. Why was Paul so adamant about preaching the Word? As you re-read the last paragraphs of Acts 28, do you get the sense that Paul was a dull and dry teacher of the Word or a passionate communicator? Why?

_____

_____

_____

6) How many references can you find in chapters 27 and 28 to believers ministering to the apostle Paul? Why is this mentioned?

_____

_____

_____

7) Why is it important to demonstrate love and support to those in positions of spiritual leadership?

_____

_____

_____

TRUTH FOR TODAY

The church in Acts faithfully carried out Christ's charge, "Be My witnesses both in Jerusalem, and in all Judea and Samaria, and even to the remotest part of the earth" (1:8 NKJV). The church has passed the baton through many hands down through the centuries to us. Will future generations find that we ran our segment of the race carefully?

REFLECTING ON THE TEXT

8) As you think back over the record of the first-century church as recorded by Luke, what impresses you most? Convicts you most?

_____

_____

_____

_____

9) In what ways does your church emulate the believers in Acts? In what ways is your congregation unlike the early church? Try to be honest. What specifically needs to change?

_____

_____

_____

_____

10) Compose a prayer that summarizes your thoughts and feelings now that you have concluded this study. What do you want to say to God?

_____

_____

_____

_____

Personal Response

Write out additional reflections, questions you may have, or a prayer.

_____

_____

_____

_____

_____

_____

_____

_____

_____

_____

_____

_____

_____

The MacArthur Bible Study Series

Revised and updated, the MacArthur Study Guide Series continues to be one of the bestselling study guide series on the market today. For small group or individual use, intriguing questions and new material take the participant deeper into God's Word.

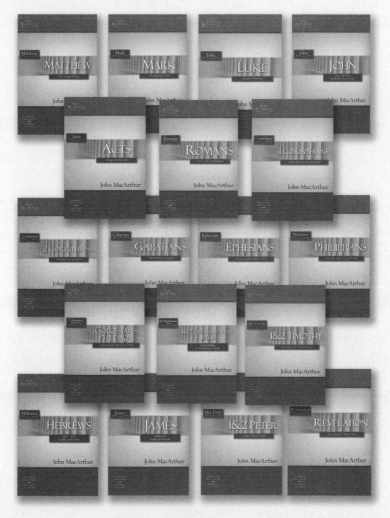

Available at your local Christian Bookstore or www.thomasnelson.com

THOMAS NELSON

Since 1798

thomasnelson.com